Lives of the Australian Chief Justices

SIR WILLIAM A'BECKETT

Lives of the Australian Chief Justices

J. M. Bennett

New South Wales

Sir Francis Forbes
Sir James Dowling

Victoria

Sir William a'Beckett

Lives of the Australian Chief Justices

SIR WILLIAM A'BECKETT

First Chief Justice of Victoria
1852–1857

J. M. BENNETT
M.A., LL.D.

Foreword
The Honourable Michael Kirby, A.C., C.M.G.
A Justice of the High Court of Australia

THE FEDERATION PRESS
2001

Published in Sydney by

The Federation Press
71 John St, Leichhardt, NSW, 2040
PO Box 45, Annandale, NSW, 2038
Ph: (02) 9552 2200 Fax: (02) 9552 1681
E-mail: info@federationpress.com.au
Website: http://www.federationpress.com.au

National Library of Australia Cataloguing-in-Publication data:
Bennett, J. M. (John Michael)
Sir William a'Beckett: first Chief Justice of Victoria

Includes index
ISBN 1 86287 409 3

1. a'Beckett, William, Sir, 1806-1869. 2. Judges - Victoria - Biography. I. Title. (Series: Lives of the Australian Chief Justices).

347.014092

Typeset by The Federation Press, Leichhardt, NSW.
Printed by Ligare Pty Ltd, Riverwood, NSW.

Foreword

(By the Honourable Justice Michael Kirby, A.C., C.M.G.)

In this life of Sir William a'Beckett, John Bennett takes the reader back to the early years of the Australian colonies. They were years severe for just about everyone. There was a thin veneer of civilization; but it barely masked the passions of power, lust, greed and vengeance.

Dr Bennett portrays his subject as a man with many admirable qualities. He persevered despite a mysterious spinal disability that would have laid low a lesser being. Although the bearer of the name of the famous English saint and Lord Chancellor, he ventured to the new, uncertain colony in Sydney to try his hand as a lawyer in rustic circumstances. His ambition for judicial preferment soon took him to Port Phillip. He presided over the trials of many colonial *causes célèbres*. He conceived of himself as a person duty bound to give moral leadership to the colonists, living with him in what one of his Sydney legal colleagues described as "the dismallest and most desolate hole a civilised and social being could be buried alive in". And, at the last, he returned "home" to England to be buried without ceremony in the Norwood cemetery. At the time of his interment in 1869 it was close to the Prince Consort's dazzling Crystal Palace, where the colonial "nonentity" doubtless spent many an interesting hour of his short retirement. Now his grave lies in an undistinguished burial ground of suburban London, not far from the scene of the Brixton race riots of a few years back that would have shocked this valiant apostle of stable British governance and law and order.

But who was the *real* William a'Beckett? It is of the nature of Victorian colonial grandees that they took pains to hide their personal feelings and deep emotions. Almost certainly a'Beckett suffered grievously under the unloving regime of his solicitor father, said to have been the model for the unyielding Ralph

Nickleby penned by that sharp observer of the English legal scene, Charles Dickens. The young William was probably brutalised at the Westminster School, known for its bullying that was thought to develop the heroic spirit that built the Empire. He was an outcast who left his native land to travel to a place as remote from his family and friends as he could possibly go. As John Bennett observes, he never really felt himself to be an Australian. He was obliged to perform public duties under the vituperative commentary of an unfriendly press and the unyielding meanness of colonial officialdom. Even at the end he was cheated out of the full pension which he had been led to expect if he resigned to permit his impatient successor to seize the judicial central seat. He imposed on himself a stern discipline both in his judicial life and his personal affairs. He wanted, desperately, to set a high moral standard. He took his Christian religion seriously. He wrote poetry. When he lost his wife he remarried her sister. He became a leader in the teetotal movement. In his last years he suffered the ultimate indignity of seeing a son who should have been a comfort to his old age, virtually elope with, of all people, a brewery owner's daughter.

One puts this book down with a feeling that its subject did not have much joy in his life. Mostly, his life was about service and duty, ambition and achievement. Yet it was lived in the way that was expected of those who, in the nineteenth century, were bringing British justice to the four corners of the world - and, in particular, to Australia. Here is a typical imperial judicial officer of whom it could truly be said - he did his duty. He was not inspired. But, then again, he was not expected to be.

And yet, is there more? Dr Bennett portrays a'Beckett, the young man, as a skilled advocate; as a judge who quickly mastered the arcane world of equity law and was unafraid to press it into newer fields; and as a man who struggled against physical infirmity that plagued him for most of his adult life. He shows how a'Beckett stood up for the rule of law against the hectoring of the local press and the passions of the mob who cheered jury verdicts in favour of populist leaders or causes. In fact, a'Beckett emerges as something of a bulwark against the demagogues of those early colonial circumstances and as a generally fair and accurate judge - even in the trial of the Eureka defendants. He normally erred, if at all, on the side of humanity and mercy. In the age when the death penalty elevated judges to a super-human power over the very lives of their fellows, he was an important example of honest service. And behind that public face was a man who struggled to be a minor writer of literature and was distressed at what he saw as the greed and dislocation caused by the gold rush that would eventually elevate Melbourne, after his departure, to be the glittering jewel of the new land.

Views will differ, as they have in the past, over a'Beckett's conduct of the Eureka trial and the trial of George, son of that humbug John Dunmore Lang. Other writers have criticised a'Beckett's rulings in those trials - especially the former. But Dr Bennett suggests another viewpoint. It is convincingly argued. By dipping into the actual transcripts and court and press records, he allows us to evaluate for ourselves how well this judge - described by his son as a conservative tory - managed his judicial obligation of impartiality in circumstances where popular temperatures were high and passions frayed.

The most enduring message of this book is the way - virtually from the start of Australia' colonial history - the elements of a rule of law society were built by people such as a'Beckett. After the American Revolution of 1776, there would be no more supine subservience or unquestioning obedience to authority on the part of the British settlers beyond the seas. The Australian colonialists wanted self-government, elections and jury trial. And they wanted them now. It was a'Beckett's privilege to take a leading part in the colonies in those early days of law and justice. The role he played was overwhelmingly honourable. He left the institutions of law stronger than he found them. We are the inheritors of what he and his contemporaries built.

We are also indebted to John Bennett for bringing those times to life and for showing how the stream of justice and law in Australia is a continuous one. William a'Beckett was there, virtually at the beginning. He did what was expected of him, and perhaps more. His contemporaries were not very grateful. Looking back, with Dr Bennett's help, we can be more charitable.

Michael Kirby

CANBERRA

1 September 2001

Contents

Acknowledgements

This project, to write of the lives and careers of nineteenth century Australian Chief Justices, originated many years ago. It was inspired by discussions with my mentor in legal history, Dr C.H. Currey, when he was completing his great work *Sir Francis Forbes* (1968). My project took its first shape when I held, briefly, a Senior Research Fellowship in the Law Department (now Program) of the Research School of Social Sciences within the Australian National University. Encouraged, first, by Professors Geoffrey Sawer and S.J. Stoljar, the enterprise has commended itself, in turn, to Professors Paul Finn (now the Honourable Justice Finn of the Federal Court), John Braithwaite and Peter Cane. Much of my research has been conducted in Canberra and the association with the A.N.U. has been sustained by several visiting appointments. The more pressing calls of professional practice conspired, however, to delay excessively the completion of my writing.

For a private author, the cost is daunting of undertaking a project of such a scale as is this series. Much research must be pursued at a distance from home, often inter-State or overseas. I gratefully record my indebtedness to the Law and Justice Foundation of New South Wales for sponsoring my initial research. I acknowledge the personal interest of successive Foundation Directors Terence Purcell and Simon Rice, and of Grants Managers Dawn Wong, Steven Reynolds and Catherine Lloyd.

Later research was assisted by the award of a 2000 Churchill Fellowship, a recognition I am privileged to have received. It enabled me to examine sources in the United Kingdom, Bermuda and the West Indies. I much appreciate the assistance of the Winston Churchill Memorial Trust in facilitating the necessary travel, and I particularly thank Mrs E.L. Munday, O.A.M., Assistant Executive Officer to the Trust, for her help with administrative matters in relation to the grant.

My attempts to understand and interpret the personality and private thoughts of Sir William a'Beckett would not have travelled far had it not been for the generosity of his descendants. Family papers and records have been placed at my disposal and permission readily given to publish quotations from them. For that invaluable assistance, much of it given a decade ago, I thank Mr E.C. a'Beckett, barrister and solicitor, of Aldinga, South Australia; Mrs W.A.K. a'Beckett of South Yarra, Victoria; Mrs P. Rose of Davidson, New South Wales; and Mrs N. Allworth of Wellington, New South Wales.

On the kind introduction of J.D. Merralls, A.M., Q.C., of Melbourne, Mr Charles Francis, Q.C., gave me the benefit of his expert knowledge of the history of Victoria's early legal profession, and read and commented on drafts of some of my chapters. I am most grateful for his suggestions. At a preliminary stage of my writing I was greatly assisted with suggested fields of research by Dr Brenda Niall of Monash University and by Bryan Keon-Cohen, now Q.C., then of the same university.

Preparation of the book has taken me to many libraries and archival sources. I particularly acknowledge the patient assistance of the staff of the La Trobe Library within the State Library of Victoria, and of the National Library of Australia, Canberra, A.C.T. In 1990, James Butler, Librarian of the Library of the Supreme Court of Victoria, kindly permitted me to inspect unique holdings in that collection and to publish quotations from them. My isolation from metropolitan centres has caused me to make heavier than normal demands on the inter-library and microform facilities of Bowral Central Library. I record my thanks to the Inter-Library Loans Officer, Anne Howe.

I am indeed fortunate to have this volume so handsomely introduced by the Honourable Justice Kirby of the High Court. His interest has not been confined to my work on Sir William a'Beckett but has been continuous across the years that my "Lives of the Australian Chief Justices" has been taking shape. I thank him for his encouragement of the project when, at times, it seemed a task almost too great to accomplish. And, for similar encouragement, I renew my best thanks to Mr Chris Holt of the Federation Press.

MITTAGONG N.S.W. **J. M. Bennett**

August 2001

List of Illustrations

(facing pages 82 and 83)

"*Dramatis Personae*"

[A brief introduction to the principal actors]

a'BECKETT, William, London solicitor, father of Sir William.

a'BECKETT, Sir William, in New South Wales: Solicitor-General 1841-1843; Acting Judge of the Supreme Court 1843-1845; Resident Judge, Port Phillip 1846-1852. In Victoria: first Chief Justice 1852-1857. The subject of this book.

BARRY, Sir Redmond, Commissioner Court of Requests 1843-1851; Solicitor-General 1851-1852; Judge of the Supreme Court 1852-1880.

BURTON, Sir William Westbrooke, Judge of the Supreme Court of New South Wales 1832-1844.

CROKE, James, Clerk of the Crown for Port Phillip; Crown Prosecutor from 1841; Solicitor-General 1852-1854.

DOWLING, Sir James, Judge of the Supreme Court of New South Wales 1827-1837; Chief Justice 1837-1844.

FORBES, Sir Francis, first Chief Justice of New South Wales 1823-1837.

GIPPS, Sir George, Governor of New South Wales 1838-1846.

GREY, (Henry) George, third Earl, Under-Secretary (Political) for the Colonies 1834-1835, 1835-1839.

GURNER, Henry Field, first solicitor in Melbourne; Crown Solicitor 1842-1880.

HOTHAM, Sir Charles, Lt-Governor of Port Phillip 1853-1855; Governor of Victoria 1855.

KERR, William, newspaper editor, proprietor of the *Argus* (Melbourne) 1846-1848, an outspoken critic of Sir William a'Beckett.

LANG, Revd Dr John Dunmore, Presbyterian cleric, political activist and promoter of controversy.

LA TROBE, Charles Joseph, Superintendent, Port Phillip 1839-1851; Lt-Governor 1851-1854.

MICHIE, Sir Archibald, barrister in Sydney 1841-1849, in Melbourne from 1852; Attorney-General 1857-1858, 1870-1871; Victoria's first Q.C.

MOLESWORTH, Sir Robert, Acting Chief Justice 1853; Solicitor-General 1853, 1855-1856; Judge of the Supreme Court 1856-1886.

PAKINGTON, Sir John, Secretary of State for the Colonies 1852.

POHLMAN, Robert Williams, barrister and diarist, Commissioner Court of Insolvency 1847; Master in Equity 1851; Commissioner Court of Requests 1852; first County Court Judge in Victoria 1852-1877.

PLUNKETT, John Hubert, Solicitor-General of New South Wales 1832-1836; Attorney-General 1836-1856; Australia's first Q.C.

STANLEY, Lord, Secretary of State for the Colonies 1841-1845.

STAWELL, William Foster, Attorney-General 1851-1857; as Sir William, Chief Justice (in succession to a'Beckett) 1857-1886.

STEPHEN, Sir Alfred, Judge of the Supreme Court of New South Wales 1839-1844; Chief Justice 1844-1873.

THERRY, Sir Roger, Commissioner Court of Requests (New South Wales) 1829-1844; Resident Judge, Port Phillip 1844-1846; Judge of the Supreme Court of New South Wales 1846-1859.

WILLIAMS, Sir Edward Eyre, Chief Commissioner of Insolvent Estates 1851; Commissioner Court of Requests and Chairman of Quarter Sessions 1851; Solicitor-General 1852; Judge of the Supreme Court 1852-1874.

WILLIS, John Walpole, Judge of the Supreme Court of New South Wales 1837-1841; Resident Judge, Port Phillip 1841-1843.

1

Running Away From Home

"A Family Quarrel of the Most Painful Character"

Sir William a'Beckett did not trouble much about his ancestry, but for his father, as for his own eldest son W.A.C. a'Beckett, genealogy was a compulsive study. "People ... generally ask: 'Are you descended from St Thomas a'Becket?", wrote W.A.C. a'Beckett.[1] Of course, without violating his vows, the sainted Archbishop had no direct descendants. As the *Dictionary of National Biography* more cautiously put it, the family claimed "descent from the father of St Thomas a'Becket, archbishop of Canterbury".[2] The father of Sir William (also named William) wrote a "Sketch of the Ancient Family of a'Beckett of Wiltshire", which claimed that, in the 12th century, "St Thomas a'Beckett was the son of Gilbert a'Beckett ... by Matilda, the daughter of a Saracen Prince, to whom he had been captive in love while a Crusader".[3]

Martin Boyd, the author, was an a'Beckett descendant and made use of family memoirs and history as a foundation for some of his novels. Sir William a'Beckett is supposedly the model for Boyd's characters "Sir Henry Montfort" and "Sir William Langton". Boyd's interweaving of fiction with fact has been unravelled by Dr Brenda Niall, in *Martin Boyd – A Life,* a study that makes any detailed review of a'Beckett genealogy otiose in these pages.[4] But a summary will set the stage for what follows. The family appears to have been established in England at the Conquest, with branches named "Becketts", "Beckets", "Beckotes" or "Bekks", one of which, styled a'Beckett, was prominent in

Wiltshire from about the 16th century. William a'Beckett, who lived from 1483 to 1565, had his home at Littleton in Wiltshire and was the ancestor of seven successive generations of [a']Becketts, each eldest son being named William.[5] Thomas a'Beckett, who was born in 1722 and died in about 1790, has been described as "a scion of the a'Beckett family long settled" in Wiltshire.[6]

By the marriage of that Thomas to Philippa Turner, there was born, on 7 June 1751, at Littleton Panell, another Thomas a'Beckett. After schooling at Marlborough College, Thomas, the younger, entered Brazenose College, Oxford, where he attained the degree of Master of Arts in 1778, going on to holy orders in the Church of England. At various times he was Vicar of West Lavington in Wiltshire, "Clerk Curate of Wootton Underwood in the County of Buckingham" and domestic chaplain to the Duke of Buckingham.[7] Before graduating at Oxford, this Thomas had also mastered the arts of fathering two children, (one of whom died in infancy), by Martha Nicholls, the daughter of a farmer. The publishing of banns and the solemnization of matrimony appear not to have attended the union. The child who survived was a son named William. He was born on 11 April 1777 at Doverdale in the County of Worcester.[8] He, in turn, would be the father of Sir William, the subject of this book.

The gentlemanly status of the Revd Thomas was exalted in 1851 when, on the death of his younger brother Gilbert (High Sheriff of Wiltshire), he became entitled to a substantial Wiltshire property called the Penleigh estate. It happened thus. In March 1788 Martha Turner, sister of Philippa a'Beckett and widow of George Turner of Penleigh, made her last will.[9] It contained a "name and arms clause" of a kind then fashionable in wills or settlements affecting real property. Such a clause enabled a testator to impose on the taker of an estate the obligation to assume the testator's surname and to bear his arms. The condition could not be imposed upon a tenant in fee simple and thus had the effect, if accepted, of entailing the estate. Names and arms clauses required "the utmost nicety in framing"[10] and similar nicety in acceptance. It was not permissible to assume the surname as part of "a double-barrelled name":[11] hence Thomas could become Thomas a'Beckett Turner, but not a'Beckett-Turner.

Martha Turner had been carefully advised about her will. It conferred a benefit on her a'Beckett nephews, not by seniority, but on other grounds. Thus Gilbert Trowe a'Beckett was the prime beneficiary; on his death without male heirs the estate would pass to his elder brother the Revd Thomas, and on Thomas' death without male heirs, the estate was to go to the youngest brother William. The intention probably was to preclude any possibility that Thomas' illegitimate son might acquire title as a *bastard eigné*, whereby the eldest son born out of wedlock could sometimes succeed to real estate. On Martha's death, Gilbert acquired Penleigh but, on his untimely death without heirs, the title passed to Thomas who assumed the style Thomas a'Beckett Turner. On his death, in 1838, the grotesque laws of bastardy, that penalized the innocent victim of supposed scandal, allowed the estate to go over to Thomas' younger brother.

Thomas evidently provided his son with an education and the means of launching himself, in due course, in practice as a London solicitor, William having first entered into articles of clerkship in 1790.[12] Relations between father and son cannot have been close. Thomas made no provision whatever for his son when disposing of his personal property by will in 1835.[13] William, the son, shielded himself from the stigma of the bend sinister by assuming only the patronymic a'Beckett, and immersing himself in the history of its lineage. The circumstances of his upbringing undoubtedly influenced his own remote awkwardness as the father of a large family to be mentioned shortly.

William's career, although eclipsed by the brilliance of his progeny, was eventful. In addition to his law practice, he had served with the rank of Captain in the St James Volunteer Corps (later the Queen's Westminster Volunteers), was "a strenuous supporter of municipal reform", a leader in parochial reform at the Church of St James, Westminster, and a lobbyist against the detested "Window Tax".[14] Dr E.G. Coppel, Q.C., in an originative paper on Victoria's first Chief Justice, observed that William, the solicitor, was "a remarkable man" who,

> held radical political opinions during the Napoleonic Wars. He was one of a small number of solicitors who founded the Law Society which eventually took charge of the legal education of solicitors. But he had a violent temper, was emotionally unstable and at one time suffered a serious, though temporary, mental breakdown.[15]

At St George's Church, Hanover Square, on 17 February 1801, he had married Sarah Abbott, "one of a very large family, the children of . . . the proprietor of a glass and china warehouse".[16] William a'Beckett eventually lived at "The Grange" in Hampstead, but, when William the younger (the eventual Sir William) was born, on 28 July 1806, the father lived and had his professional office in Broad Street, Golden Square, near Piccadilly.[17] After primary schooling at the academy of a Miss Turner, young William went from 1816 as a "half-boarder" and, later, with his brothers Thomas and Gilbert as "home boarders", to Westminster School. It was, wrote W.A.C. a'Beckett:

> In the good old days of fagging, fighting and Greek and Latin verses and nothing else; other subjects not being thought fit for gentlemen. . . He was, while there, one of the most physically vigorous in the school; was one of the most constant and best fighters and cricketers, and had several well-remembered and severe fights.[18]

Westminster School was "world renowned" for the brutality of bullying permitted there, from which Gilbert in particular, who was a frail and sometimes sickly child, suffered acutely. Turning in desperation to his father to intercede with school authorities, Gilbert found that "the old martinet . . . treated the appeal with contempt" and would do nothing.[19]

It is true that young William was articled to his father for several years, but it is not true, as W.A.C. recorded, that his decision to read for the Bar was attributable to a dream of William's mother that he would be a judge some day.[20] The prosaic reality was that William, the solicitor, was a severe father whose patience was often stretched by the exuberance of his young family, and whose pockets were being emptied in trying to educate them. He was disposed to periods of anger and of "not speaking" when things went wrong. The son Gilbert, who became very friendly with Charles Dickens, was convinced that his confidences to Dickens about the demeanour of the father had inspired the character Ralph Nickleby, "the stern old man", in Dickens' *Nicholas Nickleby*.[21] William, the younger, from childhood had stood up to his father. Others in the family long remembered his successful remonstrance "We went away because you beat us unjustly, and if you beat us again, I will run away again".[22]

Working in his father's office, the son's mind was rather on Latin verse and English prose than on conveyances or writs, and he "paid very little attention to the business carried on there".[23]

The father rankled, the son chafed, and there was soon a falling out:

> [The] father positively refused to give him any pecuniary assistance in any shape or form, the result being a family quarrel of the most painful character culminating in [the son's] leaving the paternal roof, and taking up his abode with his maternal aunt, [Mrs Hayley]. . . Thrown entirely on his own resources, he sought literary employment, and succeeded so far as to take chambers in Serjeants Inn [but] his life [was] one of continuous anxiety of the most heart wearing character.[24]

He entered at Lincoln's Inn on 15 November 1822 and secured his call to the Bar on 30 June 1829.[25] His father then softened a little and inscribed and presented to William the copy of Jacob's *Law Dictionary* (9th edition 1772) that had been given to him on entering into articles.[26] But paternal briefs for the new barrister there were none. Without his father's patronage, work was hard to find but, as mentioned in more detail later, his literary qualities triumphed and ensured him a living. He had gratified his interest in the arts by spending nine months in Italy soon after being called to the Bar.[27] The adventure enhanced his ability to work as a writer and, back in London, he assembled capital enough to marry his aunt's daughter Emily, at St Pancras Church, on 1 October 1832,[28] there being three sons of the marriage born between 1833 and 1836. The marriage seems to have stimulated a reconciliation between the solicitor father and son and, although the former did little to further the son's English career, he was the means of directing the son's progression to Australia.

William, senior, was the English solicitor for Dr Robert Wardell, a pioneer of the New South Wales Bar, and a newspaper proprietor in England and in the Colony. Wardell's *Statesman* in England was, at the material time, managed by a man named Fisher who was friendly with young William and who, on the murder of Wardell in 1834, suggested that the Sydney Bar would suffer Wardell's loss keenly and that attractive opportunities for new lawyers were open in New South Wales. The advice was taken, a brother-in-law advanced £500 towards the passage money, and the a'Becketts, with their three young sons, sailed for Sydney in the *City of Edinburgh* late in 1836.[29] They had not sailed far when a "most terrific hurricane" dismasted the ship which was laid up at Plymouth for several weeks. After that false start, the journey was resumed and the family arrived at Port Jackson in May 1837.[30] William a'Beckett was admitted to the colonial Bar on 1 June 1837, on the motion of J.H. Plunkett, the Attorney-General, and a future rival for judicial office.[31]

A "Most Eloquent Advocate"

Commencing, no doubt, with introductions from Fisher, a'Beckett found that the Sydney Bar offered him a very good living indeed. Sir James Martin, the fourth Chief Justice of New South Wales, recalled him as being the Colony's "most eloquent advocate before the arrival of Mr [Robert] Lowe".[32] Being immediately in demand and earning good fees, a'Beckett set himself the goal of making fortune enough to return at least £300 per year to each of his sons for their lives.[33] He said that he averaged £2000 a year in his first four years (equivalent to the stipend then received by the Chief Justice), which rose to £2300 when augmented by his salary as Solicitor-General from his appointment in 1841 with a right of private practice.[34] He had good reason to be grateful for Fisher's advice in directing his path towards so great a change in fortune. During his stay in Sydney a'Beckett successively occupied at least three residences, one of which, "a very commodious dwelling" at Newtown, he called "The Grange" commemorating, with surprising sentimentality, the name of his father's house.[35]

According to Dr Coppel, Q.C., the case that launched a'Beckett's Australian career was *Faunce* v. *Cavenagh*, in March 1838, an action for libel against the then proprietor of the *Sydney Gazette* by Captain A.T. Faunce, a Police Magistrate of Queanbeyan, formerly of Brisbane Water, himself no stranger to litigation.[36] Believing that he was following the wishes of Governor Bourke to curb cattle stealing, Faunce had behaved so excessively as a magistrate at Brisbane Water, in disposing of such cases, that he was sued by some of those on whom he had purported to inflict extreme punishments, and was himself mulcted in such severe damages that he had to sell his military commission. George Cavenagh caused the *Gazette* to reflect on the behaviour of Faunce who instituted the subject proceedings in defamation. So successful was a'Beckett, in his defence of Cavenagh, that the jury, although finding for Faunce, awarded damages of only one farthing.

In 1838, trials, resulting from the "Myall Creek Massacre" in northern New South Wales, brought a'Beckett's name into even greater prominence. He was one of a defence team of three counsel, William Foster and Richard Windeyer being the others. They were retained by subscriptions from many rural landowners. The case has attained modern significance because of the brutality with which a group of assigned convict labourers, all white men acting without provocation, rounded up and slaughtered many members of an aboriginal community camped by Myall Creek.[37] Eleven of the convicts were eventually apprehended, taken to Sydney, and put on trial before Chief Justice Dowling and a jury. The defence team claimed that no victim of the alleged crime could be identified: indeed, mutilation of the bodies rendered that impossible. The jury accordingly brought in a verdict of not guilty that caused spontaneous delight within the court room and received almost universal approbation among the white colonists. The Chief Justice, whose summing up lent no support to an acquittal (as a'Beckett would no doubt later recall when he presided at the Eureka Trials in Victoria), had great difficulty in controlling the court.[38] Only the courage and high sense of justice of Attorney-General Plunkett caused a reversal by the bringing of new proceedings, before Mr Justice Burton, charging the murder of one identified child. A plea of *autrefois acquit* was put to a jury which found as a fact that the new charge differed from those for which the accused had been acquitted. In the result, despite public uproar, the defence failed, petitions for clemency were rejected, and the offenders were hanged.[39]

In days when egos and honour were easily bruised, and direct retribution seemed, in the heat of the moment, a better resort than going to court, a'Beckett had some lucrative briefs arising from the practice of horsewhipping a traducer. Two cases attracted particular public attention.

In the first, in October 1840, he represented "Major" James Mudie, plaintiff in an action against John Kinchela, junior, seeking damages for a violent assault. Mudie, a large landowner in the Hunter district, was unpopular, and had made many enemies, in high places in the Colony.[40] They included Chief Justice Forbes and Dr John Kinchela (former Crown Law Officer and, briefly, a Supreme Court Judge). In his unrestrained *The Felonry of New South Wales*, published in 1837, Mudie attacked the characters of Forbes,

Kinchela and many other prominent colonial figures. Kinchela's son thereupon took to Mudie with a horsewhip, and in consequence found himself defending Mudie's court action.

The jury awarded Mudie damages in the significant sum of £50, which was "promptly paid by subscription in the court".[41] Why the jurors were swayed by a'Beckett's advocacy is difficult now to fathom, as much of it has the appearance of empty rhetoric of no obvious relevance. For example:

> The evidence of past history, and the record of modern events, combined with reflection upon both, had convinced him [a'Beckett] that the person who entertained such sentiments [as were summarized in the adage "*Vox populi, vox Dei*"], stood upon dangerous ground, which was liable, every moment, to give way under his feet. Could the maxim be appropriately applied to the excesses, so bloodthirsty and revolting as to make the heart sick at their base contemplation, committed in France at a period within the recollection of many?[42]

In the second instance, where his advocacy was more direct, but the result went against him, a'Beckett (acting privately, though then in office as Solicitor-General) was matched against Attorney-General Plunkett representing the plaintiff. The case, *Wilson* v. *Christie*, came to trial in June 1841. It was another example of bruised vanity and injured honour, which arose out of the Australian Club's annual elections. Henry Croasdaile Wilson, a former colonel in South America, had been appointed as Sydney's first Police Magistrate, but was controversial in, and eventually suspended from, that office.[43] In 1841 he stood for election as the Australian Club's secretary/treasurer, but was defeated by Major William Harvie Christie.

Stung by his failure, Wilson published anonymous newspaper articles suggesting mismanagement of the club's affairs, and reflecting adversely, so Christie concluded, on the virtue of Christie's wife. Preferring direct action, Christie sought out Wilson and struck him "with an unmanly and unprecedented ferocity".[44] Formal challenges followed, but a duel was averted only by Wilson's inability to find a second. Admitting publication, but denying that he had referred to Mrs Christie even by implication, Wilson sued Christie in the Supreme Court for assault. a'Beckett attempted a long and "most eloquent" defence, (so the *Sydney Herald* reported), in which he urged the jury to disregard the efforts of Plunkett "to inflame them with one of his usual elaborate and political speeches".[45] The jury instead found for the plaintiff and awarded damages in £150. The young Irish barrister Thomas Callaghan, sitting in court in the hope of a brief, and appearing to be busy by taking notes, recorded in his diary that a'Beckett had made "a very spirited speech but he did not speak as *feelingly* as I expected".[46]

In criminal proceedings, the services of a'Beckett continued to be much sought. In February 1841, for example, he had a convincing victory in defending William Roemer on charges of obtaining under false pretences a promissory note drawn by the "brewer, miller, hotelier, whaler, shipper, and large-scale merchant" (eventually declared bankrupt) John Terry Hughes.[47] The defence relied on absence of proof of intent and on glowing testimony as to the good character of the accused. The verdict of not guilty must have been the more acceptable to a'Beckett as the prosecution had been conducted by Foster, whom he personally disliked. Two days previously, however, he had been obliged to appear with Foster, jointly conducting a successful defence of two men charged with forgery.[48]

Later that year a strenuous exchange occurred between Plunkett and a'Beckett, on opposing sides in *Lettsom* v. *Boyd*, the hearing of a criminal information in which Major Lettsom charged Archibald Boyd, a New England grazier and barrister by call at Lincoln's Inn,[49] with "wickedly, maliciously, and illegally sending [him] a challenge to fight a duel". The parties were self-important to the point of absurdity as the facts revealed. Outside Cox's Hotel in Maitland, a group of men had assembled, Boyd and Lettsom among them. Boyd complained to Lettsom, "Sir, you look at me very hard". After further pleasantries, Lettsom rejoined, "I can look at any body I like; . . . if you don't like to be looked at you had better lock yourself up".[50] The following day Boyd sent a messenger to Lettsom demanding an apology. It was not given. A demand for a duel was then made, which Lettsom also refused – "he had nothing to fight for". Boyd retorted, by mail, that, failing an apology within a limited time, "he would feel himself under the necessity of posting [Lettsom] at his Club in Sydney, and at Cox's and Cohen's Inns at Maitland, as a coward and no gentleman". The time having expired, Boyd acted on the threat. The prosecution followed.

Plunkett, insisting that he acted as a private advocate, appeared for Lettsom and claimed a right of reply after a'Beckett "had indulged in such strong terms of animadversion on the conduct of his client". Chief Justice Dowling intervened to assert that Plunkett, having used "some very strong expressions" against the character of an absent party, was in no position to reflect on the defence. When a'Beckett further resisted Plunkett's claimed right of reply, the Chief Justice said that Plunkett might reply if he wished "but he did not think he would be exercising a sound discretion in doing so". Plunkett held his peace, and a'Beckett had the last word, deploring the bringing of criminal proceedings that precluded Boyd from giving evidence on his own behalf. He acknowledged that Lettsom had admitted to being near-sighted, which might have explained his seeming to stare, but which could not explain his "coarse and insulting language", including the abhorrent word "damn", and thoroughly dishonourable conduct.[51]

The jury, much influenced by this resort to high principle and gentlemanly standards, found Boyd guilty. But only, they said, because the Chief Justice had directed them that they were bound by law so to decide. They added a rider that Boyd's conduct had been "under circumstances of great provocation, irritating conduct, and coarse language of the prosecutor" which recommendations to mercy they pressed upon the court. It took very little to provoke a duel or a prosecution in those days!

From 1840 a'Beckett's life took a varied course. Professionally, he laid the foundation for his advancement to the judicial Bench. But domestically and personally he experienced some bitter times. The robust health of his youth failed him and he first became aware of a gradual paralysis that made walking, and even standing in court, progressively difficult without assistance.[52] His doctors could not explain the condition, but his brother Thomas was convinced that it originated in a spine injury due to an accident sustained while playing cricket at Lords.

> He struck out to hit a ball aimed at his wicket and, missing it, swung himself round so violently as to fall to the ground, where he remained for about a minute, unable to raise himself. When he did so, he was so wretched as to be unable to continue the game. . . He . . . did not entirely recover his power of locomotion for nearly a fortnight.[53]

The disability, in due course, played a part in influencing his decisions to seek, and ultimately to retire from, a judicial appointment.

The first two of his colonial children died in early infancy. Another son was born in 1840, but the young family was desolated when Emily a'Beckett died suddenly on 1 June 1841 after complaining, as William left for court that morning, of "a strange feeling about her head, which she could not account for". Thomas Callaghan attended the funeral, the service being, as he wrote, "read by a conceited histrionic actor of a fellow of the name of Steele". Callaghan recorded his sense of pity for a'Beckett "for he has been kind to me".[54] Mourning his loss, a'Beckett composed an eloquent Latin epitaph for his wife, that survives them both.[55] But there was little time for grief as the management, not only of his practice, but also of his household of young boys, had come to fall wholly on him. For one about to assume new public responsibilities he found himself facing unusual domestic tasks. He wrote, of his children, that "they are beginning to get particular about dress, and there is no end of bother now . . . [but] I don't mind this. I remember that I was [the same myself] – and let them have what they like".[56]

At the very height of his Bar career, in 1841, a'Beckett invited Callaghan to join him at a family meal. Callaghan listened intently to all dinner table conversations and recorded many of them. On this occasion, he wrote that his host was "a man of rather kindly nature tho' he seems to have been poor and really thrown on the world: he is of *very* delicate frame and is sickly". More engaging was a supposedly confidential discussion they had about personalities at the Sydney Bar. According to the diarist, a'Beckett said:

> That he did not like either Therry or Foster: that neither of them were sincere or to be trusted – he is right: he said he thought Hustler would never do here and that Purefoy made a terrible mess of a pleading which he had drawn a few days before: he said that when he came here first he thought Broadhurst was a coxcomb but that now he liked him: he said that he liked Plunkett and Windeyer who were men of honor, and that my friend Darvall was a cold heartless man.[57]

The claimed regard for Plunkett would later be stretched to breaking point, as will emerge.

Only three weeks before his bereavement it was made known that a'Beckett would act as Solicitor-General while Plunkett, then in that office, took overseas leave for 18 months:[58] a'Beckett had entered on the office temporarily some months earlier. Chief Justice Dowling, in October 1840, wrote to a'Beckett, expressing his "entire approbation", hoping that the Secretary of State would confirm the appointment, and remarking, "The office which you now hold is most responsible. It requires a man of high principle, considerable knowledge of the law and of its practice, united with temper, discretion and good sense. These are qualities which I certify you possess".[59] Alfred Stephen, then a puisne judge, added his congratulations and considered the appointment a tribute to a'Beckett's merits. While he thought it would add little either to immediate fame or emoluments, Stephen, with an eye to the future, advised: "Do not too much despise rank even though only *Colonial* rank. It will confer on you the means of more extended usefulness. Every added source of influence is important, and with you will be valued as enabling the possessor to do good to his fellow men".[60]

Dowling seems to have been as intrusive, in his support for a'Beckett, as he would become in virtually nominating Stephen as his successor in the office of Chief Justice.[61] Roger Therry, who had come to the Colony in 1829 as Commissioner of the Court of Requests, suffered, like Plunkett, the disadvantage – in the context of colonial society – of being a Roman Catholic. Each man paid a heavy price in New South Wales for adherence to his religion. Therry, although sharing a'Beckett's literary interests, was offended that a'Beckett, a newcomer, had so rapidly attained a foothold on the ladder of preferment. Therry wrote to his friend the former Governor, Sir Richard Bourke:

> I had been recommended for the office of Solicitor-General both by Sir F. Forbes and Sir J. Dowling long previous to Mr a'Beckett's arrival in the Colony. I had subsequently been recommended for that office by yourself . . . and Sir George Gipps [who] further recommended me himself for the office of Solicitor-General, which did not succeed, . . . he has preferred Mr a'Beckett's claims to mine and I confess freely to you, I feel *humiliated* and *wronged* by this preference.[62]

Therry attributed the preference wholly to religious favouritism. He grumbled, with justification, that there could be no rational connexion between a Crown Law Officer's religion and his official duties that had nothing to do with Church affairs.

Otherwise, for the time being, good will prevailed, and, at a large dinner party for him, in March 1841, Plunkett declared:

> When I know that the duties I had the honour to conduct are now transferred between two friends, Mr Therry and Mr a'Beckett (vehement cheering for some seconds), I perceive their well known reputation and personal character is such, that in the transfer of the public duties into their hands, that public will be no loser.[63]

Lord Stanley, later in 1841, declined to affirm a'Beckett's appointment, given that the previous administration had refused to revive the office of Solicitor-General in New South Wales "until the several Establishments of the Colony had been reduced". Before that advice was received, Sir James Dowling, then in rapidly failing health, had sought leave of his own and had warmly recommended a'Beckett's elevation as temporary puisne judge, testifying to his experience in practice, his "good sense, discretion and ability" and his acceptability to the legal profession and to the public.[64]

Meanwhile Governor Gipps had made such strenuous representations for revival of the Solicitor-Generalship that Stanley relented in 1843, confirming not only the office that a'Beckett had since filled *de facto*, but also a'Beckett's occupancy of it.[65] Apart from a few interests in which he took a public position, especially the temperance movement and concern for underprivileged people, a'Beckett confined himself to the duties of Crown Law Officer and to his permitted private practice. There were rumours that he might seek to involve himself in the political affairs of the Colony, but, with one exception, he always resisted taking that step. The exception occurred in 1844 when Gipps, anxious to get an extra supporter into the fractious ranks of the limited Legislative Council, prevailed on a'Beckett to become a nominee member. The manoeuvre was crudely mismanaged. Sir Maurice O'Connell, Commander of the Forces, agreed to Gipps' request that he yield up his seat to a'Beckett. Once done, it was only then realized that O'Connell held his place *virtute officii*: "no successor to Sir Maurice could be appointed, unless he were also Commander of the Forces, and as Mr a'Beckett was not prepared to accept, nor Sir Maurice to resign that office, the latter resumed his seat, and the former escaped the unsought distinction of a government nominee".[66]

In the result, Gipps was doubly embarrassed, for the discovered illegality extended also to Attorney-General Plunkett's Council seat, and the matter had to be cured by the intervention of the Colonial Office. Never again did a'Beckett have any direct part in politics.

"An Implied Promise of Preference"

Port Phillip, although earlier settled informally, was given official recognition in September 1836. With few settlers at first, justice, such as it was, could be administered by arbitration and, from 1838, by Courts of Petty Sessions. A Court of Quarter Sessions was convened in 1839, but major cases had to go to Sydney for determination by the Supreme Court - the whole of what is now Victoria then forming part of New South Wales.[67]

The *Administration of Justice Act* 1840 (N.S.W.) (4 *Vic. No.* 22) made many changes to colonial law and legal arrangements. For present purposes its significance lay in its constituting the office of Resident Judge at Port Phillip and giving him a remarkable jurisdiction to exercise the powers of all or any of the Judges of the Supreme Court.[68] There was a virtual appeal to the Full Bench at Sydney, but the Resident Judge was not eligible to sit in review of his own decisions.

The prompt filling up of the office owed less to solicitude for the inhabitants of Port Phillip than it did to accommodating the wish of Governor Gipps to remove from Sydney a most troublesome judge, John Walpole Willis. His unjudicial behaviour reduced the new regional court to the level of a dramatic theatre. An apologist of Willis' career in Port Phillip, echoing an opinion of Sir Redmond Barry, has written that Willis was "sadly misjudged" and should be assessed as a man of principle who did "much good work", including showing sympathy for the underdog in litigation. On that view:

> He was hard working, independent, of unimpeachable integrity and staunchly concerned with the impartial administration of the law. He did much to clean up the community and to help overcome the mercantile difficulties which had engulfed it.[69]

Nevertheless, his conduct in Sydney had been appalling, and he succeeded, in Melbourne, in alienating the support of all those who mattered most. As Professor A.G.L. Shaw has pointed out, the greater difficulties "arose not from [Willis'] attitude on matters of law but from his personal behaviour".[70]

Determined to restore decorum to that court, Governor Gipps precipitately removed Willis from the bench through a purported "amotion" under the *Colonial Leave of Absence Act*. Finding a replacement judge was not easy. Gipps, in 1842, offered the position on a temporary basis to a'Beckett who declined it "upon mature consideration of all the circumstances". Chief Justice Dowling then intervened to propose the name of William Montagu Manning, then Commissioner of the Courts of Requests, whom he regarded highly,[71] while resisting Gipps' notions of despatching Mr Justice Burton to the south. Gipps instead appointed William Jeffcott who entered upon the office, but eventually resigned it on what he saw as a matter of principle.

> Willis having appealed to the Privy Council against his removal from office, in December 1844 Jeffcott insisted upon resigning because of conscientious scruples, not shared by anyone else, that his appointment as judge might turn out to have been invalid if Mr Justice Willis' appeal should be upheld.[72]

Willis did succeed in his appeal, on a technicality rather than on the merits. It was a hollow victory. His removal was ratified and he was offered no other judicial appointment. The Melbourne vacancy then went, in 1845, in partial gratification of his sustained lobbying, to Therry, circumstances having dictated in Sydney a game of musical chairs on the judicial bench that must now be examined.

Sir James Dowling, exhausted by his duties as Chief Justice of New South Wales, died on 27 September 1844. In June of the same year William Westbrooke Burton, a Judge of the Supreme Court since 1832, had left Australia to take up a promotion for which he had long striven - appointment to the bench at Madras.[73] He hastened there, and to the associated knighthood he so much coveted, with scant concern for the predicament his departure would cause in Sydney. Alfred Stephen remained as the only judge able to carry on the business of the court. Sir John Dickinson was yet on his way out from England to replace Burton, while Plunkett, unprepared to vacate his Legislative Council seat and cause pending criminal prosecutions to be "deranged", declined an invitation to become a temporary judge.[74] Plunkett miscalculated his position and seriously prejudiced his future interests. Gipps turned to a'Beckett who accepted the temporary judicial position in July 1844 with a sense of physical relief, for his paralytic infirmity was making it progressively harder for him to remain on his feet for long periods as counsel in court. Nevertheless, a'Beckett wished it to be remembered that he had been motivated by a desire to serve the public interest in quitting a secure position for an uncertain one, and "on the understanding that my declining would embarrass the Government and that my position as Solicitor-General was considered as giving Your Excellency a claim upon my services, under [which] circumstances, I threw no impediment in the way of the proposed changes".[75]

Dowling's death changed the relationship between leaders of the Bar among themselves and with Alfred Stephen (whose earlier patronage, by Dowling, the Sydney Bar already resented). There was a fierce contest between Plunkett and Stephen for the Chief Justiceship, in which Stephen eventually triumphed. While the contest raged, a'Beckett, who had been recommissioned (much to Therry's dismay) in a temporary capacity from 21 October 1844, following Dickinson's arrival, anxiously considered his options. If Plunkett became Chief Justice, the bench of three would have its full complement. But if Stephen were raised from puisne judge to Chief Justice there would be a judicial vacancy. On 3 October 1844 a'Beckett wrote at great length to Gipps asserting his claim. He was entitled to consideration, he said, because of the temporary judicial duties he had undertaken on "an implied promise of preference".[76] In default he sought the Attorney-Generalship. He contended that, as between himself and the Colonial Government, "all precedent" favoured his claim and was against that asserted by Plunkett. A briefer letter to Lord Stanley summarized his grounds, pointing out "the very serious injury I must suffer by returning to the Bar at all, after an absence even of the shortest duration".[77] Therry, not yet translated to Port Phillip, opposed a'Beckett's alternative claim to be Attorney-General, while complaining that a'Beckett's temporary judicial commission should have been offered, not to him, but to Therry.[78]

Plunkett heard of a'Beckett's representations "with considerable astonishment". The man whose admission to the Bar he had so recently moved, had turned out to be a cuckoo in the legal nest. Plunkett protested that an unintended and unacceptable public construction had been placed by a'Beckett on private and confidential conversations between them. The only one of them that could have been "tortured into a hint that I would resign in [a'Beckett's] favour or anyone's favour" arose out of the first news of Dickinson's appointment to succeed Burton:

> I considered it a reflection on me that it was not offered for my acceptance; that I could only attribute it to the circumstance of my being a Roman Catholic and, though it was unjust towards me, its operation was also prejudicial to him and the rest of the Bar . . . [and] that I would even resign my office in this Colony in exchange for one elsewhere rather than be the innocent cause of injury to other members of the Bar.[79]

He considered his past friendly association with a'Beckett to have been abused. He asserted that a'Beckett's appointment as Solicitor-General had been made on Plunkett's own recommendation coupled with strong representations made in England when a'Beckett "had no friend to speak for him at the Colonial Office but myself". In particular, Plunkett did not like a'Beckett's Westminster School style of fighting: "I solemnly declare that, if it were to procure me the Office of Lord High Chancellor of England, I would not use such means to accomplish it, as Mr a'Beckett has descended to, in order to obtain the seat he now fills".[80]

While a'Beckett's manner of proceeding cannot be commended, obtaining judicial advancement in the British Colonies was not for the tentative, and the state of a'Beckett's health contributed much to the sense of urgency and determination with which he applied himself to the contest. Plunkett, in turn, stretched credibility by claiming to have been a'Beckett's virtual patron. The latter had already won esteem in the eyes of Governor Gipps, and had a family, of influence, able and willing to intercede for him at Whitehall when necessary.

Gipps, perplexed by the many difficulties and opposing claims, was relieved to commit their resolution to the Colonial Office. Because of delays in communications, the matter took time to be settled. With Therry's removal to Melbourne as Resident Judge in February 1845, the Sydney Bench continued *pro tempore* with Stephen as acting Chief Justice, Dickinson as senior puisne, and a'Beckett clutching grimly to his temporary commission.

Gipps tried to be even-handed. He said that, "in preferring the claims of Mr Alfred Stephen and Mr a'Beckett to those of Mr Plunkett and Mr Therry, I had done violence to my own feelings",[81] but he also conceded that to have appointed Therry ahead of a'Beckett "would have been ungracious towards Mr a'Beckett, and might have produced a bad effect in the Colony".[82]

As the months passed in waiting for the Colonial Office's answer, all parties became increasingly unsettled. Gipps decided, by October 1845, that he must do something definite. He reported to the Secretary of State that:

> After a great deal of trouble, and playing at cross purposes, I have proposed on the part of the Government, and for the convenience of the public, that Mr Plunkett, Mr Therry and Mr a'Beckett all remain where they are for *12* months. Mr a'Beckett objected (and I think with reason) to any arrangement of the sort for less than 12 months.[83]

Stephen had resisted unsettling those arrangements. Already, on the bench, a'Beckett had made an invaluable contribution in managing equity suits, the complexity of which did not commend them to his judicial colleagues. As a ground for retaining a'Beckett as a Sydney judge, Stephen represented to Gipps that:

> The Equity business . . . now demands, more than ever, the most able and efficient superintendence. It is right to say that Mr a'Beckett's great knowledge and experience as an Equity lawyer, increased during the term of his judicial service by most unwearied and industrious study, cannot in this Colony be equalled.[84]

In more recent times, Dr Coppel, Q.C., and Dr Pannam, Q.C.,[85] have drawn attention to a'Beckett's embracing, in 1845, the supposedly modern doctrine of constructive trusts, in *Walker* v. *Webb*. The judge was undeterred by the lack of precedent authorities, insisting that "if the present case is new, its novelty is no reason why the Court should not deal with it, and, if necessary, mould its decision according to its peculiar exigency".[86] In all respects, a'Beckett had demonstrated ability and independence as a Sydney judge, doing nothing to warrant the suggestion once made that, in those days, he suffered from "a vacillation of purpose, and a proneness to be unduly influenced by colleagues".[87]

2

Moving to Melbourne

"We Have No Friends Here"

At last, on 6 September 1846, the decision of the Colonial Office reached the Governor after the despatch had been five months on the high seas. In the meantime a'Beckett continued to complain "bitterly of being kept in a state of suspense".[1] The future lives of the supplicants were ordered in the space of three concise paragraphs. Lord Stanley could "perceive no reason" for setting aside the provisional appointment of Stephen as Chief Justice. It was confirmed, and Dickinson therefore ranked as senior puisne. Plunkett's aspiration to be Chief Justice by virtue of being incumbent Attorney-General was denied, but the third place on the bench was to be offered to him.[2] Plunkett first prevaricated, then declined in a sense of dejection and disgust.[3] Therry was nominated as the next entitled to the vacancy, having regard to his long service "and the high testimony borne in his favour on repeated occasions".[4] He accepted with alacrity. It remained for a'Beckett to choose between a permanent appointment as Commissioner of the Court of Requests or "the Provisional Judgeship" at Port Phillip, subject to confirmation of the latter depending on the outcome of the appeal by Willis to the Privy Council.

As a'Beckett's hero poet, John Milton, wrote in another context, the occasion was one where the "high arbiter Chance governs all".[5] Therry rushed, jubilant, back to a place on the Sydney Bench that, as it happened, afforded him little ultimate satisfaction. In doing so he cast aside the opportunity, all but inevitable with the benefit of hindsight, to become the first Chief

Justice of Victoria.[6] On the other hand, a'Beckett took courage to spurn the secure offer of tediously mundane work in the Court of Requests and to see what destiny might offer him in Melbourne. Sydney's legal profession farewelled him with genuine good will at a well attended dinner.[7]

The Melbourne Bar then matched neither Sydney's numbers, ability nor fraternity. At the beginning of 1846 there were only six of them. The "queer old Crown Prosecutor, often as uncouth in his tongue as in his general demeanour"[8] was James Croke – whose name Charles Dickens might have invented. Then there were Brewster, Barry, Pohlman, Williams and Stawell. Robert Pohlman, who kept a diary, seemed more interested in noting the picking of the season's first grapes than in saying much of "our new judge" on his arrival by the *Shamrock* on 7 February 1846. Therry, however, was at the wharf with "most of the officers of the Supreme Court" to receive the newcomer.[9] Bar comity no doubt enabled the two to meet on outwardly civil terms, despite their intense private rivalry. Four days later the Bar gave a dinner, Croke presiding, rather to farewell Therry than to receive a'Beckett, though he was there, as was Superintendent La Trobe (soon to become Lieutenant-Governor). Pohlman thought that Murray's Prince of Wales Hotel had done little for the occasion – "Dinner bad in every respect; want of attendance, respect and attention".[10]

On 16 February a'Beckett took his place on the bench for the first time, being assisted to his seat by the Sheriff. He appeared to be "in very delicate health", and observers thought that he must have had some rheumatic condition. Fortunately it was Melbourne's first maiden assize, only Croke and Pohlman being in court, and the occasion became the merest formality in which the judge's commission was read.[11]

So far from having been "anxious to remove to Port Phillip" as J.L. Forde put it in his *Story of the Bar of Victoria*, a'Beckett went "much against his own inclination" and at first shared Therry's loathing of the place.[12] The new judge wrote to the Sydney solicitor B.C. Rodd, "we have no friends here. Perhaps we may yet – I don't like this place and never did quite".[13] He protested to Lord Stanley that the new office had severed him "from all my friends and associations".[14] Archibald Michie, then a rising member of the Sydney Bar, attested that he knew what a'Beckett had "suffered in his official removal from Sydney [to] . . . the dismallest and most desolate hole a civilized and social being could be buried alive in".[15] Yet there was no time to brood. The temporary Resident Judge had to consolidate his position and was at once at work on a submission to the Colonial Office that he conceded was of "a length not very usual, and perhaps not very welcome, in official correspondence".

He made much of the sacrifices imposed on him by transferring to Port Phillip:

> I had formed connexions and associations . . . I had relations too who had come out from England to be near me; [Sydney] had become my home; my wife lay in one of its churchyards; my children were being educated there, and my character, both private and judicial, was known and valued by all whose good opinion was worth having.[16]

He further represented that the Sydney Bar had become so large that he could not easily retrieve his former place. If he were to go back to practice, he would lose his seniority and find it stultifying to have to plead before the very bench of which he had been a judge. His position had become "hazardous and humiliating", so he said, and, if displacement from Port Phillip should be his lot as the result of Willis' appeal, he begged for an equivalent judicial appointment elsewhere. He hoped, though, that such a move would not become necessary. He could foresee an imminent Victorian separation from the original New South Wales, "in which event there might be advantages connected with the judicial office here". He forthwith staked a claim to be Chief Justice of any new southern Colony.[17]

Gipps warmly supported a'Beckett's representations.[18] But chance again intervened when, despite Willis' success on his appeal, his removal from office was allowed to stand and, changes having occurred in the respective Imperial and Colonial administrations, Earl Grey advised Governor FitzRoy, in October 1846, that a'Beckett was confirmed in the permanent office of Resident Judge.[19] Therry, sensing perhaps the force of a'Beckett's forecasts about separation and a new Chief Justiceship, hastened to have his judicial seniority over a'Beckett officially recognized after the *London Gazette* had announced, in alphabetical order, their respective appointments.[20]

The confirmation in office enabled a'Beckett better to order his domestic arrangements. He bought a house in Collins Street, Melbourne, and sometimes rusticated at St Kilda, described thus by Michie from an observation in about 1847:

> I was informed that he was at St Kilda, about three miles on the southern side of the Yarra. I trudged off – 'buses and low-backed cars were unthought of in those days . . . I soon found myself in a pretty thick bush, and reached St Kilda, which, so far as I could judge, seemed to . . . consist of one house . . . on the shore. In this house I found my friend [a'Beckett] amongst some of the members of his family, seated on a dingy and battered old sofa, with a patient perseverance that almost brought tears into my eyes, as he endeavoured to persuade himself that he was spending a few days, at what he called, with the utmost seriousness, a watering-place.[21]

There then began the tiresome business of doing battle with officialdom about the cost of becoming a regional judge. It was bad enough to have to pay the fees and stamp duty on the warrants for his commissions. But the government as well demanded the refund of £100 it had advanced towards his removal expenses.[22] He was incensed. No earlier Resident Judge had had to pay his own way to get to Melbourne.[23] Moreover, he insisted, he held only the titular office of Resident Judge: his various commissions had all been as a Judge of the Supreme Court of New South Wales. He asserted that, under s. 4 of the *Administration of Justice Act* 1840, the Governor was empowered to direct a judge to go to Port Phillip and that he had been so directed by Gipps "not because any vacancy had occurred there, or because I had applied to go there. It was not my act or wish: on the contrary, I remonstrated against it".[24]

He further complained about injustices. He had had to sacrifice his furniture by sale to reduce the actual voyage cost from £200 to £115. On 22 January 1846, T.S. Mort had auctioned a'Beckett's "elegant household furniture" at his residence, then in Castlereagh Street, Sydney, including a "large-sized miniature theatre with scenery, machinery, lamps & characters, etc.", many musical instruments, and even a "teapot, richly chased, & moulded with a kangaroo in frosted silver".[25] FitzRoy felt satisfied that the judge had shown sufficient reason why the government should not press its financial claim. The Colonial Office thought otherwise.[26] FitzRoy yielded to a'Beckett's urgings to seek a reconsideration, and transmitted another verbose remonstrance by the judge, which took the point that, if the Secretary of State would not reconsider, he might at least authorize the Governor to place the sum on the colonial estimates so that the Legislative Council could assess the merits of recovering it. The Colonial Office would not budge. The minute paper recorded that "though Mr a'Beckett has complicated the question by throwing in a great many circumstances he has not added anything which really serves to strengthen his claim".[27] The answer was "No", and the judge had to pay.

A happier conclusion to this part of the story occurred on 30 October 1849 when a'Beckett remarried. Among the relatives to accompany him to Melbourne had been his late wife's sister Matilda. Although not technically illegal in New South Wales to marry a deceased wife's sister, the union fell within the Table of Kindred and Affinity prohibited by the Church of England. According to Thomas a'Beckett, "Bishop Perry personally was strongly in favour of such a marriage and issued in my brother's case a licence to the Rev. M. Newham to solemnize the marriage in my brother's private residence".[28] The marriage was successful and brought great comfort to a'Beckett as his physical strength continued to ebb because of his gradual paralysis.

"Our Much Respected Resident Judge"

The first task of the new judge was to win the respect of the Melbourne Bar. Croke, its seemingly indomitable leader, had ruled the roost, holding his own even in the court of the abrasive Willis. More than once he had led a "walkout" of the Bar, effectively preventing Willis from continuing court business.[29] Therry considered Croke to be "a diligent upright officer", but a'Beckett found him to be troublesome and temperamental, and their relationship was strained.[30]

Pohlman recorded attending a dinner on 8 July 1847 that La Trobe gave, most incongruously, almost a year after a'Beckett's arrival, and several months after the judge's confirmation in office, to enable the Bar to "meet" the Resident Judge. It must have been a thoroughly uncomfortable and poorly planned occasion:

> At dinner ... in addition to the Bar (less [Sidney] Stephen) were Majors Reeve and St John which greatly disconcerted the party – the

> Judge and Croke, Croke and Barry, Croke and self, Williams and St John not being on the best of terms it was the heaviest of our dinners there.[31]

The rift between the judge and Croke was traceable to "a fracas in court" between a'Beckett, Croke and Stephen in the preceding March. Croke called a meeting at his chambers "to consider the Judge's animadversions upon him at the last Criminal Sessions". The Bar, however, felt that they could not, as with Willis, act in concert and they resolved that the matter was Croke's sole concern as Crown Prosecutor.[32] Croke, thereafter, was not always invited to a'Beckett's parties for the Bar.

Edmund Finn captured the diplomacy with which, in public, a'Beckett secured mastery over the Crown Prosecutor:

> One day [Croke] and Chief Constable Sugden were "barneying" about some hitch in a criminal case. Their recrimination attracted the attention of the Judge, who, looking determinedly at both the offenders, exclaimed "Mr Croke, it would be extremely inconvenient for me to have to commit the Crown Prosecutor for contempt during the Criminal Sessions; but (turning to Sugden) if the Chief Constable *does* not hold *his* tongue, I certainly shall commit him".[33]

Croke was not readily tamed. In March 1848 the *Albion* reported a "flare-up" in court following Croke's resort to unfair cross-examination in his "intense anxiety" to secure a conviction. When the judge reproached him, Croke thundered that public justice was being defeated.

> "Pray Sir", said his Honor, "who are you alluding to in making that remark", "Pardon me, your Honor", said Mr Croke, "I feel strongly", and with his hand on his breast the learned gentleman humbly bowed . . . and was about stammering out an apology when his Honor himself put a stop to the scene by remarking in a kindly tone, "You should not allow your zeal Mr Croke to attempt to strain evidence to a pitch which I cannot allow".[34]

By firmness a'Beckett came to command the Bar's respect and, allowing for the clashes inevitable in contentious litigation, acrimony and personality were usually foreign to his court. He encouraged *esprit de corps* among the Bar, holding dinners at his home, sometimes with "theatrical representations", and he attended reciprocal gatherings in the residences of barristers.[35] Pohlman, who participated in many of them, and who became a confidant of the judge and, at one stage, executor of his will, was hurt at being passed over when a'Beckett had important visitors as dinner guests – Sir Alfred Stephen, Richard Windeyer and Deas Thomson among them.

In the conduct of his court, a'Beckett, whether as Resident Judge or later as Chief Justice, habitually exercised judicial restraint, but his demeanour was not always predictable. While usually a model of detachment and sometimes displaying good humour, he could become irritable especially when unwell. There were times when he seemed distracted to the point of eccentricity. Newspaper records traced his changes of mood. Undoubtedly they were influenced by the debilitating course of his paralysis which was probably aggravated when he was thrown violently from his carriage, in April 1848, on the breaking of its axle-tree.[36] Three months later he had enjoyed a perceptible recovery: Pohlman wrote that "the Judge and I walked from his house to the Court this day". But, by 1850, the judge was unable to walk at all and he depended on using a wheelchair to get about. Lack of mobility weakened his general health exposing him to colds and other infections. An influenza epidemic in 1849 laid him low, incapacitating him for a time from conducting the court, and leaving him "very poorly".[37]

A striking example of the judge's sense of distraction occurred in July 1849 when Susan Mullins (alias Susan White) was indicted for the stabbing murder of William Kelly. Croke conducted the Crown case in accordance with the indictment but, when he had closed, to "the astonishment of the Court and spectators", a'Beckett summed up to the jury as on a case for manslaughter. His clerk, R.W. Shadforth, rose in embarrassment to point out that the case was one for murder.

> His Honor – Charged with murder?
> The Clerk of the Court – Yes, your Honor, the indictment is for murder.
> His Honor – For murder; I was not aware of it; I thought it was for manslaughter.[38]

The judge, described by the *Argus* as being "very confused", claimed not to have heard the indictment clearly read, and insisted that the case was in the list as one for manslaughter. This time Croke intervened, to spare a'Beckett great humiliation, and suggested that the judge's address to the jury had advanced such circumstances of mitigation as to justify the lesser charge. The case was put to the jury on that basis and, luckily for the prisoner, a verdict of guilty only of manslaughter was returned.[39] The incident occurred soon after a prolonged and bruising contest between a'Beckett and the editor of the *Argus*, the details of which are mentioned shortly. It is plain that ill health and preoccupation with the *Argus* had left the judge in a sometimes wandering state of mind.

Other instances of a'Beckett's judicial demeanour will be noticed later. Two examples are mentioned here from his period as Resident Judge, illustrating his strong views on insobriety and other vices. On one such occasion the press reported that:

> There was such an intolerable smell of smoking [in the court] that his Honor ferociously enquired for the delinquent, and threatened "to put his pipe out". It turned out, however, that it was not in the body but immediately outside the court. . . His Honor always careful not to overstep the bounds regretted much that his authority did not extend so far, or most assuredly he would have committed the smokers.[40]

While, historically speaking, courts were never kind to jurors who could not reach expeditious agreement, a'Beckett, on one occasion in 1849 when he directed a discordant jury to be locked up overnight, was concerned to ensure that their confinement should be kept "dry":

> The Foreman – Will your Honor allow us refreshments?
> His Honor – As you will have to remain until the morning, there is no objection to your having bread and butter and tea, *but no wines or spirits*.[41]

As to a'Beckett's judicial style, it was reasonably said in the *Melbourne Weekly Herald* that, if he displayed any leaning, it was on the side of clemency and humanity.[42] A surviving Register of Remissions of Sentence held in the Library of the Supreme Court of Victoria confirms that a'Beckett's recommendations to mercy were far more liberal than was then the general custom. Death sentences for various serious crimes were often, on his recommendation, commuted to lesser penalties. He was even instrumental in having a sentence of transportation within the Colony overturned and a free pardon substituted.[43] His moderate course was not unanimously applauded. In an angry article, the *Albion* which, in its short career, constantly attacked weaknesses it perceived in the legal system, contended that:

> In our last issue we expressed a fear that the extremely lenient sentence passed by our much respected Resident Judge, who at all times displays an anxious desire to temper justice with mercy, upon the two Burkes for an aggravated assault upon some constables in the execution of their duty . . . would operate rather prejudicially to the preservation of the peace in this province. Subsequent events have proved that our fears were well grounded.[44]

There was the appearance of leniency of another kind which the Port Phillip press was quick to condemn. In October 1849, the *Geelong Advertiser*, immediately seconded by the *Argus*, deprecated what it described as a "game of 'Fast and Loose' " between the magistrates and the Resident Judge as to committals in criminal cases.[45] It complained that, despite the closest attention given by those preparing process in criminal matters, the judge constantly allowed accused persons to escape because of technical slips in the documents. But no consistency could be extracted from his rulings. Sometimes, it was claimed, he would reject a warrant for departing from the words of the statute, but at other times for following the statute too closely. In this "game", wrote the *Advertiser*, the magistrates and other court officers "always come off beaten; the Judge is always too quick for them, and having the privilege of the last word, is sure of scoring a victory". It protested that the administration of criminal justice was being paralysed by a judicial preoccupation with minute technical niceties.

In the then recent case of a prisoner named Wall, the warrant charged that he had knowingly concealed 13 gallons of illicit spirits "against the form of the Act". The decision of a'Beckett, J., was that the quoted words should have been preceded by the phrase "liable to forfeiture", which, as the *Advertiser* pointed out, found no authority in the Act itself. On the judge's construction of the warrant, the process was discharged and the prisoner released. The *Argus* concurred that the number of failures of prosecutions on procedural grounds was as considerable as it was capricious. It deplored "the endless dismissals ... which have formed so remarkable a feature in the administration of justice by Mr a'Beckett".[46]

Although, at the outset, the duties of the office were so slight that a'Beckett recalled of them that he exchanged bows with his associate "and that was generally the amount of business",[47] the district's changing circumstances soon caused him to be fully occupied. Even before the gold rush began, there was a perceptible growth in crime, while the court was increasingly resorted to by civil litigants with complicated commercial and property disputes for resolution.

Regarding his judicial duties with solemnity, a'Beckett delivered reserved judgments of considerable substance and much greater regard to precedent authorities than was usual at the time. Between 1846 and 1851 he published annually (from 1847 in the name of his clerk Shadforth) his *Judgments of the Supreme Court of New South Wales for the District of Port Phillip*.[48] With that work and his *Reserved and Equity Judgments of the Supreme Court of New South Wales During 1845*, which won unstinting praise from Chief Justice Alfred Stephen,[49] a'Beckett may properly be described as the founder of systematic public law reporting in Australia.[50] Sir James Dowling's extensive manuscript reports of New South Wales decisions remain unpublished in printed form. The contribution of M.H. Stephen, in 1851, was confined virtually to cases on practice points.[51] Legge's Reports, though including cases dating from 1825, were compiled and published many years later in reliance on old newspaper material. Coming today to peruse the Resident Judge's reported decisions, one is struck by the dearth of cases on matters of public law. The great constitutional issues that weighed upon the courts in Sydney and in Hobart were absent from early Melbourne. It was relatively a backwater in which the administration of the criminal law and the resolution of private litigation were dominant.

The principal exceptions were some cases about local government. In 1851 a'Beckett gave judgment in *R.* v. *Young; Ex rel. Hepburn*,[52] in which it was sought to oust David Young as a Councillor representing FitzRoy Ward and to have John Watson declared elected in his place. Young had succeeded in the December 1850 election by only four votes. Watson sought to show that 12 votes had been received improperly. Personation and the lapsing of residential qualifications were the chief grounds relied upon, but they were so poorly presented – not even the electoral list and voting paper form being in evidence – that a'Beckett, while conceding that the issues were "neither frivolous nor groundless", disposed of them shortly:

> The Court must have before it a *prima facie* case, supported by something like legal evidence, and not by mere suspicion, hearsay,

> or conjecture: nor by conclusions of law drawn from facts which are not stated at all, or so loosely as not to afford any ground for determining whether such conclusions are correct.[53]

A more substantial foray into public law was *In re John Thomas Smith*,[54] a decision of 1848, dealing with entitlement to be entered on the "burgess roll" for local government elections. Smith, describing himself as a "yeoman", had won Bourke Ward in the first Melbourne Town Council in 1842: "He was a 'Whittington of the South', being seven times mayor between 1851 and 1864".[55] In 1848 confusion arose over Smith's qualifications to be on the roll because of the nature of properties (including a tavern and a theatre) that he relied upon as his residential nexus with Bourke Ward. In a political gesture, his name had been expunged from the roll. In the Supreme Court he sought a *mandamus* compelling the restoration of his name so as to ensure his right to vote and, as a candidate, to avoid prospective challenges should he be elected.

The Resident Judge did not grant the *mandamus*, but he managed to do justice all round. The objections, which had been raised by a notice issued to Smith himself, were declared invalid because the notice did not follow the statutory form in scope or substance. Smith's position was held equally to be insupportable because he had not shown that his title as an elector had been proved or even offered to be proved before the intermediate Revision Court. It was for that tribunal, not for the Supreme Court, to determine his eligibility and only if it expunged his name on grounds shown to be wrong in law could the superior court intervene. Moreover, Smith had not discharged his statutory obligation to show that he was a ratepayer whose rates were currently paid. In any event, his "inhabitant householdership" was not made out, having regard to the nature, and his use, of the properties on which he relied.

At the same time, those responsible for expunging Smith's name received a judicial reproach. The court had not been assisted by their failure to give evidence of their grounds. And their attempt to have the proceedings terminated as excessive were likewise condemned. To their rhetorical question "Are the extraordinary powers of the [Supreme Court] to be put in motion, merely to give Mr Smith a vote?", a'Beckett, from the bench, rejoined:

> I answer undoubtedly they are, if that vote be a right, for the denial of which the law has given him a remedy – and such remedy would be lost by delay... The Court requires no man to swear that he conceives himself damnified by being illegally hindered from exercising his elective franchise. The injury speaks for itself ... involving as it does the loss of one of the great constitutional rights, of which Englishmen are so justly jealous, and the still further extension of which not only the discontented and factious, but some of the most eloquent and highly gifted of our countrymen, are at this moment daily and hourly struggling to obtain.[56]

"A Condition of Individual Outlawry"

The decision in *Smith's Case* opened the way to another testing area – the disposition, in those days, of residents in a confined community to defame one another. Sir Roger Therry recalled of his term that the office of Resident Judge was "peculiar and ... not very agreeable" because:

> He was bound to extend, in his single capacity of judge, the protection of the law to all other persons in the community, and was himself the only person unprotected by it. The judge thus became a target for all the libels with which any unprincipled writers thought proper to vilify him. His status was little better than that of being consigned to a condition of individual outlawry.[57]

It did not take Melbourne's press long to test the mettle of a'Beckett, the *Argus*, through its editor William Kerr,[58] leading the way on two fronts. One related to the consequences of *In re Smith*. The other had arisen some months earlier out of defamation proceedings brought against Kerr by Henry Moor, solicitor, Chief Magistrate, and "Port Phillip's most prominent lay Anglican".[59] Kerr had published a scandalous commentary on Moor, the innuendo being that he was a man of low moral standing who owned public houses used as brothels, and who was unfit to be Chancellor of the new Diocese of Melbourne.[60] The jury, in proceedings before a'Beckett, after deliberating for six hours, found for Moor, awarding damages of £250, then a huge sum.[61] Kerr had his lawyers move, in the following Term, in arrest of the judgment. The Resident Judge declined either to order a nonsuit or to accept an argument that he had misdirected the jury on the question of publication. He was not persuaded by other submissions going to a request for a new trial. He refused to disturb the judgment. He agreed that one innuendo had not been made out fully, but:

> There is no ground for arresting the judgment, not only because there is a sufficiency of good innuendo, after rejecting the bad, but because also I think the libel may stand without any innuendo at all. Anything which tends to the disparagement of a man's character is a libel.[62]

The result was disastrous for Kerr: the damages and costs bankrupted him. He had to sell the *Argus*, though he continued as its editor for a time. Nevertheless he battled on, trying in three further cases to have Moor's execution against him stayed and set aside as irregular, succeeding to some extent on technicalities that prevented the testing of writs of execution in law vacations.[63]

Before that *dénouement*, Kerr had used the pages of the *Argus* openly to attack a'Beckett. Of the jury's verdict in *Moor's Case* he wrote, in March 1848, that it was "not the result of a fair trial" and that "the Judge's conduct in this matter has not tended to raise him in the public estimation".[64] He added a tart poem, "The Rake's Decision", that included the lines:

> If vice in future flourish,
>   Don't you presume to check it;
> Virtue be yours to nourish,
>   And vice leave to a'B----tt.[65]

At almost the same time, Sidney Stephen's successful contempt proceedings against Samuel Goode, publisher of the *Albion*, led to the imprisonment of the one and the effective closing down of the other.[66] The *Argus*, in announcing that a'Beckett had awarded Goode two months' imprisonment, cried "Shame! Shame! Shame! That the judicial ermine should be soiled by such a proceeding".[67] On Goode's release, the *Argus* returned to the attack, decrying the sentence as "one of, if not the most unwarrantable that has ever come under our observation". It further asserted: "The fact is, the Government ought never to have inflicted upon this community in the capacity of a Judge such an utter wreck both in body and mind, and the sooner we are relieved of the grievance the better".[68]

The *Port Phillip Herald* weighed in with an attack on Croke "for not taking up the cudgels on behalf of the Judge",[69] but the *Patriot* reckoned that that was but a mischievous attempt to widen the rift publicly known to exist between Resident Judge and Crown Prosecutor.[70] Pohlman recorded a poorly organized Bar meeting held to consider the animadversions of the *Argus*. He wrote: "A meeting of the Bar to consider whether it would not be proper to vote an address of confidence in the Judge in consequence of the attack in the *Argus*. I had not heard of it and was not present but nothing was resolved upon".[71] Ripples of the incident flowed through most of Melbourne's press for some months. The judge maintained a forbearing silence. But the last straw came in December 1848 when the *Argus* and the *Patriot* (or *Daily News* as it had recently become) gave detailed reports of intemperate observations made by Alderman Johnston in the Town Council when the consequences of *In re Smith* were under discussion.

Johnston was reported to have condemned "the petty malice of a Judge, over whom malignity and folly seem striving for a mastery". He inveighed against "a'Beckettism" and looked forward to the time when:

> In our Courts of Justice, we will have an honourable and upright Judge venerable in aspect, dignified in bearing, dispensing the law with even-handed justice, alike to all, without fear or favour, instead of the inarticulate mouthings of a malignant satyr, whose sole object seems to be, the display of his own despotic powers, in a vain attempt to fill the minds of men with fear, when he has altogether ceased to hope for their respect.[72]

Those sentiments were not shared by the majority of the Council, Alderman Greeves leading a vigorous rejoinder which deprecated Johnston's remarks. The length of the latter, and their prominent ventilation in two newspapers, outweighed the counter arguments. The judge's patience was exhausted. He announced that contempt proceedings would be instituted. Having no coadjutor with whom to consult, and Croke having repeatedly refused to prosecute the *Argus* for contempt of court, a'Beckett turned to individual members of the Bar for advice.[73] He was armed with documentary proof that Kerr was the editor of the *Argus* and therefore the person liable to be dealt with for contempt. The Resident Judge's selection of Williams and Stawell (who had appeared in recent proceedings against Kerr) and of Pohlman (briefed with Sidney Stephen on Kerr's behalf) as private advisers seems odd. Probably there was no time for wider consultation as it was the very last day of Term and immediate action was essential. Williams' view prevailed that, as a'Beckett had publicly said he would initiate contempt proceedings, he should see his intention through.[74] On the same day the judge published a rule requiring Kerr to attend and show cause why a writ of attachment for contempt should not issue. Kerr appeared in person on 9 December, by which time a'Beckett seemed content to have won a psychological advantage. Kerr was kept in suspense for several months. But, during the court vacation, the judge had made the rule absolute.

On 23 March 1849 *In re William Kerr* was listed before a'Beckett when he announced that the rule would not be enforced. The decision was a tactical reversal for a'Beckett, in the face of Kerr's persistent objection that such a rule could not be made absolute out of Term.[75] Personal consultation with Chief Justice Stephen in Sydney had decided a'Beckett that he had proceeded incautiously. The Chief Justice, so a'Beckett declared from the bench:

> Expressed so much of doubt on the point, as to induce me to determine, at once, on discontinuing any further proceedings. I may say that I am not without doubt myself as to the power of the court to carry on such a proceeding in Chambers, commenced in Term.[76]

He hoped that newspaper editors would ensure that the court would have no future need to initiate proceedings of that kind. Far from being grateful or relieved, Kerr returned to the columns of the *Argus* with venom refreshed. He described the proceedings as being a "famous farce"; the *Argus*, he insisted, would not be deterred by judicial threats "from discharging what we consider to be our duty". He deplored "an act of wanton injustice, perpetrated by Mr Justice a'Beckett".[77]

The contest was far from finished. Henry Gurner, the Crown Solicitor, instituted proceedings in the Police Court, on 3 April 1849, against Edward Wilson as proprietor of the *Argus*. The summons charged Wilson with "libel on his Honor the Resident Judge in his public capacity".[78] The charge related to the "malignant satyr" report in the issue of 1 December 1848. Despite a defence that the matter should have been undertaken by the Crown on an *ex officio* information, the Bench of Magistrates committed Wilson for trial.

The *Argus*, while seeking to squeeze every drop of public sympathy in falsely representing that a'Beckett could not avoid being judge in his own cause in proceedings of this description, was furious that the *Herald* had taken the judge's side. It jeered at the judge and at its competitor alike:

> It does not seem that, in his Honor's present crusade against the Press, he has practically profitted [*sic*] by it, for if 'ever criminal' was "sold" by the ignorance of his Counsel, Judge a'Beckett has, on this occasion, been regularly butchered by his ill-informed though over-willing tool – the *Melbourne Morning Herald*.[79]

Pohlman, writing in his diary, probably exaggerated the importance of his own part in resolving the matter. Professionally, he had an interest in seeing the *Argus* spared. He recorded that, on 14 April 1849, he suggested that the prosecution be discontinued. He argued that "the real delinquent Johnston was not thereby punished", that proceedings logically should also be taken against the *Daily News*, that "no verdict was probable from a common jury and a special jury could not be obtained" and that no one, unless brought from Sydney, could preside if a'Beckett vacated his judicial place for the hearing. Having secured Croke's alleged agreement with his views, Pohlman wrote with satisfaction, "Saw the Judge afterwards and understood it to be abandoned".[80]

The *Argus* excelled itself in recrimination. In an editorial, "The Argus Persecution", it detected a clique at work in the legal profession, directed by the Resident Judge himself, who was, it still maintained, "responsible for having instigated" the proceedings.[81] The judge might "have done" with the *Argus* for the moment, but "we have not yet done with Mr a'Beckett". It protested that the judge had "most wantonly and gratuitously broken the truce lately proclaimed between us" – a remark demonstrating that the press considered itself, if not above, then on a level of equality with, the court. It had the last word, with typical spleen, when it claimed that a'Beckett had arrived in Port Phillip with a good reputation, but had been no match for "the severe touch-stone of a sole Judgeship in a limited and excitable community". Its conclusion was unsparingly malicious:

> The position of a sole Judge, indeed, requires a weight of character, and a combination of qualities which are rarely found in any man, and which Mr a'Beckett does not possess. Steadied, supported, corrected, and confirmed by other members of the Bench, he might pass through life without blame, and without committing himself; but deprived of those supports, and with his sensitive nature exposed to wounds which ordinary natures would not feel, and to

> which they were not subjected, he is in a dangerous and unsound position, and a retrospect of the past occasions sad misgivings for the future.[82]

The *Argus* recommended the Executive Government to apply, in relation to a'Beckett, the precedent of removal that had been applied to Willis.

While it cannot be supposed that a'Beckett had handled the matter incisively or with much sense of purpose, the incident demonstrated the impotence of an isolated judge in a community accustomed to a *laissez-faire* approach to the overlap between law and politics. Even La Trobe had suffered greatly, and with no recourse to any practical redress, at the hands of the press. Alderman Johnston, in the same speech that attacked a'Beckett, had traduced La Trobe, calling him "a viceregal effigy" and a "superannuated spy": observations that the newspapers willingly made public.[83]

In more settled circumstances, relief might have been found by the judge's procuring the intervention of the Sydney Bench. Therry considered that there should have been a statute requiring "that all cases, where the rights, character, and property of the [resident] judge were concerned, should be triable in Sydney".[84] While cases of contempt of *the court* could clearly have been entertained in Sydney, contempt of the Resident Judge was another matter. But a'Beckett's stepping back from the brink of a contest, at some cost to his self-esteem, worked in the community's best interests. The *Argus*, however, despite changes of editor, continued throughout a'Beckett's judicial career to display more than enmity to him.

"The Practical Mode to be Adopted by This Court"

One of the most persistent pieces of litigation at the time, and one of interest here as touching the jurisdiction of the Melbourne court, was *Marquis of Ailsa* v. *Watson*.[85] It was a case arising out of the financial depression of 1840-1841 and concerned the purported assignment of substantial holdings of real property and stock, allegedly in the exercise of creditors' powers. In its first adjudication, after prolonged hearings, Jeffcott had declared the assignment fraudulent and void as against the plaintiffs. There were many interlocutory points determined either by Jeffcott or a'Beckett, but the main contest came on appeal to the Full Bench at Sydney, which overturned Jeffcott's decision. The Sydney bench, admittedly unfamiliar with the refinements of equity litigation, disposed of the matter, not on the basis of arguments for equitable relief but because the claim was one "of property; of *legal* right" and should have been sued upon at law.[86]

Jeffcott would have been gratified by the ultimate result in which, on an appeal by special leave,[87] the Privy Council reversed the judgment of the Full Bench and four decisions of a'Beckett, while reinstating Jeffcott's decree although with major variations. It is impossible to dwell here on the merits of the case which are merely incidental to the career of a'Beckett. But the case does raise other pertinent issues. In particular, the Full Court's superficial decision had left unresolved some important procedural problems.

Of those problems, the most significant, for present purposes, is, to use a'Beckett's words, "what is the practical mode to be adopted by this court on appeal from a decree in its equitable jurisdiction, to give a successful appellant the benefit of the decree pronounced in his favour by the appellate court?".[88] It had been suggested in argument that the wrong English procedure had been applied because "the appellate court at Sydney does not stand in the same relation to this court as the House of Lords does to the Court of Chancery". The proper procedure, it was submitted, should have been like that existing on appeal from the Vice-Chancellor or Master of the Rolls to the Lord Chancellor.[89] The ingenuity of the arguments was to be admired, said a'Beckett, but the matter called for a more pragmatic solution. The court's preference to follow English practice could not stand where that practice itself gave no clear guide how it might operate under colonial conditions. It was for the Australian court to make up its own mind as to the procedure best suited to its circumstances:

> I consider it quite open to me to determine what the practice on the point now contested ought to be, without any reference to the English Rules; and as no decision has been given on the point, nor indeed required in this Court, it is right that I should endeavour to frame such a precedent as will most easily and conveniently carry out the directions of the appellate court.[90]

Reflecting on the course taken, he considered that, to act upon a judgment of the court at Sydney, he should have some certificate, exemplified copy or notification of it.

The Sydney judges overruled a'Beckett. There was, they said, but one Supreme Court of New South Wales for the entire Colony, and the expression "Supreme Court of Port Phillip", used in the documents in the case in question, demonstrated an error. As they saw it, the nature of appeal under 4 *Vic. No.* 22 was "from the Resident Judge; not to a separate court, but to his colleagues of the more numerous Bench belonging to the same Court".[91] No Judge of the Supreme Court should require evidence of the signature or official character of any other judge being his colleague, or of any officer of the court.

While acknowledging the weight of the pronouncement against him, a'Beckett, who, in the view of Dr Coppel, Q.C., "thought he had become his own master in Melbourne",[92] maintained that he had been right in law and in practice. There was, he insisted, no realistic relationship between the respective courts, their judges and staff, that rendered comity possible in accepting signatures and the like at face value. The Port Phillip judge might never have met or even seen his Sydney "colleagues". How could he vouch for their signatures and of those of officers who might be changed from day to day without his knowledge or concurrence? "The Judge for this District", he contended, "is no more connected with the Sydney bench, than the Judge of New Zealand would have been had that place continued to be a dependency of New South Wales".

He concluded by tying up his Sydney colleagues in a logical knot of their own making. How could they rely on the unity of the Supreme Court while at once "remitting" (as they had done) their original order to Port Phillip to be enforced? There should, on the Sydney argument, have been no need to have the order of the Sydney court enforced as a standing order of the Melbourne court. He thought that the appellate subjection of his court to the Sydney court "more completely marks its distinct existence as a court, than even the statutory separation of its jurisdiction".[93] Presaging the separation of Port Phillip, he said that his difficulty was a practical one arising from "the *actual division* of the two Courts" and, while the Sydney judges had made their position plain, it fell to him to carry out the consequences of their determination in a realistic way. Further to mark his sense of dissent he adjourned the proceedings to consider what final course to adopt. Ultimately, the matter was disposed of as the Sydney judges had indicated that it should be: but a'Beckett's position in the controversy had been more soundly reasoned and convincing as to the law and practice involved than that of the Full Bench had been.

Nevertheless, the Full Bench had been consistent. In April 1845, on a motion to set aside a writ of *fi. fa.* directed by the Resident Judge to the Sheriff in Sydney, Chief Justice Sir Alfred Stephen acknowledged the anomaly "that the same Court should be holden, under the same name, at two distant places at one and the same time".[94] The Full Court in Sydney (of which a'Beckett at the time was a constituent member in hearing the relevant motion: so he came to alter his position, although his colleagues did not alter theirs) resolved that:

> The Resident Judge of Port Phillip is a Judge of the Court of New South Wales, and in that capacity has an exclusive original jurisdiction in his district, but he also has an auxiliary jurisdiction in New South Wales, and has power to issue writs of execution to the Sheriff in Sydney.[95]

So rapidly were the times changing that this strained and artificial perception of the Sydney and Melbourne courts would soon be swept away as "Port Phillip" merged in Victoria.

3

New Colony: New Chief Justice

"Warfare With This Demon Vice"

The first half of the nineteenth century ended: great changes in Victoria began. The success of the separation movement, correctly foreseen by a'Beckett, was achieved in full measure. Maintaining his detachment from politics, he had taken no public part in the popular movement most emphatically expressed in the derisory "election" of Earl Grey as a Port Phillip representative in the Legislative Council of New South Wales at the limited franchise in 1848.[1] With tactics like these, the point was made, and, by the *Australian Constitutions Act* 1850,[2] the Parliament at Westminster created the new Colony of Victoria with its own Constitution. Superintendent La Trobe was to be Lieutenant-Governor – "lieutenant" in the sense of "puisne", though not subordinate, to the Governor of New South Wales.

Although leaders of public opinion in New South Wales had long recognized the change as inevitable, others resented it and attempted some rearguard resistance.[3] The early historian H.G. Turner captured that dissent in specious but amusing terms when he wrote, "the rejoicings were largely anticipatory, and there was yet much to do before the yoke of the oppressor could be cast off".[4] After delays, separation took effect on 1 July 1851 and La Trobe was sworn in by a'Beckett at an expansive public ceremony. For the time being, a'Beckett had to continue as "Resident Judge"; his elevation as Chief Justice had other obstacles in its way.

Before considering that ultimate appointment, something must be said of the character and qualities of a'Beckett as he approached the summit of his career. In many ways he was a misfit in the Port Phillip community, being imposed on it as an outsider, making few close friends there, having little in common with La Trobe, and being restricted in his early social company to the familiar acquaintance only of a few clergymen and lawyers. In so limited a settlement, where the rights and interests of any citizen great or small might daily demand his unprejudiced adjudication, it was wise that the Resident Judge stand aloof. He did not fall readily within any of the emerging patterns of colonial society in which, it has been discerned, there were "gentlemen of good family, gentlemen by profession or commission, and gentlemen by upbringing".[5] His role was more patrician. Seeking to lead an exemplary life, he saw it as incumbent on him to exhort fellow colonists to emulate his conduct and deportment so that their own stature and that of society might be uplifted. It was a policy that seemed puritanical and therefore it attracted criticism then and since.

His most conspicuous moral platform was the temperance movement which he supported with a passion throughout his Australian career.[6] While on the judicial bench at Sydney, he had, for example, used the ceremonial opening of the Maitland circuit for 1844 to declaim against the contribution of alcohol to the court's expanded list of crime. "All concerned in warfare with this demon vice", he insisted, "are engaged in a holy crusade, and one which tends not less to the removal of crime than to the introduction of social order and domestic purpose".[7] As Chief Justice of Victoria, he would look forward to the day when legislation "will ever effectually banish from the colony the curse of intemperance with which it is so dreadfully afflicted".[8] He presided at many gatherings of temperance supporters, taking a more determined position than did some Church leaders. Great diplomacy was required, for example, when in June 1849 Bishop Perry of the Church of England was invited to take the chair at a "grand Teetotal Festival" in Melbourne's Temperance Hall. The bishop, who could detect no sin in taking alcoholic drinks in moderation, declined the invitation. A compromise was negotiated by a'Beckett under which he presided, and the bishop attended the meeting simply as a speaker against the evils of excessive indulgence.[9]

At a meeting of the Total Abstinence Society in April 1852, a'Beckett, as chairman, declared that "every case that came before him in the last Criminal Sittings, was either caused by or connected with drunkenness". That did not fully accord with other contemporary statements of his to the effect that increased crime was due almost wholly to avarice attributable by the gold rush. Nevertheless, it was his opinion:

> That not only the prisons, but the hospitals and lunatic asylums owed the larger proportion of their inmates to the vice of drunkenness, and he could not but view with regret the increase in the number of public houses. For his part, he wished there was not a single public house throughout the town.[10]

His audience responded with loud cheers.

In 1854, the Chief Justice combined his senses of verse, patriotism and abhorrence of alcohol, in a poem "The Queen! God Bless Her". The effect was so incongruous that it must have evoked responses exactly the opposite to those intended. The poem's theme was that Her Majesty should be toasted "with water alone in our glass", and its conclusion, after several stanzas, was:

> Nor if our fair Queen could but gaze on us now,
> Would our homage less deeply impress her,
> Because we had kept the teetotaller's vow
> Whilst loyally shouting, "God bless her!"[11]

As a man of strong Christian commitment, a'Beckett for much of his life was an adherent of the Church of England. But, soon after his elevation as Chief Justice, he became absorbed in the formation of Melbourne's Unitarian Church. He attended its inaugural meeting in December 1852 and, with his wife, continued thereafter as an active member of its congregation.[12] He was a generous benefactor and often chaired business meetings of the supporters of that Church, at one of which he commented on the differences in religious views that had developed between his brother Thomas and himself: "He had a brother well known as a zealous adherent to the Church of England, but he did not believe that it interfered with the most perfect fraternal intercourse; they believed each other sincere, and each accorded the liberty he felt was due to himself". He affirmed his own persuasion that "the reasonableness of Christianity [was] its chief recommendation".[13] Nevertheless, his break with his traditional tenets was striking and the subject of much comment, not always charitable, in

Melbourne's religious circles where some saw his "conversion" as heretical.[14]

He concerned himself also with the need for general public education, which he pursued with almost a religious zeal, writing that "education, the great crying want of the colony goes begging vainly for alms in the prosecution of its holy war".[15] His view was that adequate schooling was a state responsibility that must, if necessary, be supported from public revenue. He favoured the introduction of an Education Tax "levyable in such a manner as that every individual should contribute something towards the required fund". Incorporated in that schooling, he contended, should be a form of compulsory religious education.[16] Until 1853 he took a leading part in the work of the Mechanics' Institution and School of Arts, and contemplated giving a series of lectures under its auspices. But, in delivering the annual report for 1852, he declared that he had changed his mind because "there had been but a thin attendance" at other Institution lectures. The progress of the body did not please him: the lectures were generally "too high for the majority of members to understand", while, at the other end of the scale, the library had degenerated into a collection "almost entirely of novels".[17]

The same spirit of encouraging his fellow citizens to nobler things extended to his denunciation of the evils he perceived in the gold rushes. They began in 1851, first luring fortune hunters to New South Wales and soon to even richer fields in rural Victoria. The a'Beckett homiliary, published as a pamphlet under the pseudonym "Colonus",[18] could have done nothing to deter the frenzied hordes of gold seekers. But it survives to tell something more of the author's character. He considered the entire fabric of colonial life to be threatened by the attendant lottery spirit that accompanied gold fever. Again he saw the issues at stake as if they were a "battle" against God by the forces of "Mammon", in which the latter succeeded in degrading the community and assailing "the foundation of the manners, not to say the morals, of civilized and domestic life".[19] His concern was less with the winning of gold itself than it was with the public perception that wealth could be won in abundance with little toil. That perception, he believed, encouraged people to demean the "work ethic" and to feel no obligation to contribute to the wellbeing of society. Dr Geoffrey Serle concluded that:

> This is more than the usual cant, so common at the time and in all ages, of the established gentleman who deplores the lust for wealth of the lower classes while blind to similar greed in his associates. Sir William a'Beckett placed cultural values above all worldly things.[20]

Less convincing is the conclusion of Professor Clark that a'Beckett was a reactionary figure, over sanctimonious, "a fanatical temperance man" whose judicial independence was likely to be compromised by those views, "an old world representative of a higher culture", committed in all respects to maintaining an elite class and determined to suppress the reasonable expectations of "real" Australians born-and-bred.[21]

Upright moralists of the Victorian age tend, through later eyes, to have "holier than thou" attributes no longer much esteemed. It would be wrong to go further, in this instance, and ascribe to a'Beckett conscious policies of foisting on an unwilling colonial community his preconceived ideas of class or politics. In his private life he had scrupulously kept clear of both. Moreover, his presence in Australia had no element of a crusade. He came, not to impose his will on anybody, but to enable himself to make better provision for his family than he could have hoped to have done "at home". Given many adversities he had suffered in Australia in his private life, not least his constant struggles against his failing health, and the virtual social quarantine into which judicial life had forced him at Port Phillip, a'Beckett should rather be assessed as a man of fortitude and of genuine good works who had tried, in his own way, to improve the lot of those among whom he lived. The gold rushes, however, became an obsession with him that risked creating a public perception that he might lack judicial objectivity.

"No Inconsiderable Degree of Anxiety"

Not only by legal ability, but also by fame and character, William a'Beckett was happily destined to become the first Chief Justice of Victoria.

As in his earlier judicial career, the transition to his new office was not as smooth as it might have been. The fault lay with the Colonial Office and its determination to reward the granting of responsible government to Victoria by divesting to the Colony as many administrative duties as possible. Although there was to have been a "Charter of Justice" (Royal Letters Patent) declaring the jurisdiction and powers of the new Victorian courts, the Colonial Office was weary of such things and had more pressing concerns. In May 1852 Herman Merivale wrote, and Sir John Pakington adopted the words as his own:

> It is . . . not the intention of Her Majesty's Government to grant any Charter at present. The provisions of the Act establishing the present legislative constitution of the Province were purposely framed with a view to enable the local legislature to deal as their own judgment may suggest with the whole subject.[22]

Meanwhile, those "on the spot" most directly affected by the changes, a'Beckett not the least of them, were unsure where they stood during the transitional arrangements. As early as July 1851 a'Beckett invited the attention of La Trobe to "the very peculiar position in which I find myself placed by the separation" of Port Phillip from New South Wales. It was, wrote a'Beckett, merely taken for granted that New South Wales would, in effect, release one of its judges to Victoria and that the Resident Judge should be that one. But on what secure legal foundation did the assumption rest? All that the governing Imperial Act (13 & 14 *Vict. c.* 59) had done was to provide for "the continuance of the powers, authorities and jurisdiction of the Supreme Court of New South Wales, and of the Judges thereof, in the Colony of Victoria, *until* put an end to by Letters Patent from the Queen" or by colonial legislation. In the interim, so a'Beckett deduced, he continued in Melbourne as a Judge of the Supreme Court of New South Wales.[23]

He was naturally concerned that, rather than going through a mere transition, his judicial career would lapse into a hiatus from which it might not re-emerge. Once a Victorian court was officially established, he would, in Victoria, be *functus officio* under his existing commissions. He could "hardly contemplate" that he would not be confirmed in office under some new commission, but nothing had been said or done to clarify his position: he was simply taken for granted. Accordingly, he looked to his future with "no inconsiderable degree of anxiety". Without official advice, from Whitehall, Sydney or Melbourne, he could not safely order his future or make any move "without danger to my present position".[24] He recalled his earlier anxieties when appointed only provisionally as Resident Judge.

The Colonial Office sent a soothing assurance to La Trobe that a'Beckett was not to fear for his judicial security. Yet it stopped short of doing anything specific: no warrant for the issue of the new commission as Chief Justice of Victoria was issued until seven months after a'Beckett first entered upon that office.[25] While, in the meantime, a'Beckett had fretted about his future, La Trobe did not share his concern, and reported to the Secretary of State:

> I am disposed to take it for granted that in the event of a Supreme Court for Victoria being constituted, I should act in accordance with Your Lordship's wishes, in provisionally appointing Mr Justice a'Beckett first Judge of the new Colony, under the full persuasion that it would be Her Majesty's pleasure to confirm the appointment.[26]

Gradually the new Victorian legislature addressed its attention to the court system. The court over which a'Beckett would preside was declared, by s. 9 of the *Supreme Court (Administration) Act* 1852, to be a court of record, the jurisdiction of which, by s. 10, extended to, "all civil pleas [and] all actions whatsoever, real, personal and mixed, as fully and amply, to all intents and purposes, as Her Majesty's Courts of Queens Bench, Common Pleas, and Exchequer of Pleas at Westminster or either of them lawfully have or hath in England". Section 11 conferred a criminal jurisdiction also governed by English models. In the result, the new court had powers virtually identical to those of its parent court in New South Wales, though the extent of its jurisdiction had the flexibility of being regulated by local statute not, as in New South Wales, by enactments circumscribed by old letters patent of the Crown. Section 3 of the Act contemplated that up to three judges might be appointed to the court "by Her Majesty's letters patent", though the Lieutenant-Governor was empowered to make appointments subject to the royal approval and, until those appointments were made, the erstwhile Resident Judge was to exercise all the jurisdiction, power and authorities of a Judge of the Supreme Court.

These provisions brought to an end some arrangements that verged on the intolerable. Stawell and Barry, the Crown Law Officers, wrote a joint opinion in 1851 recommending prompt legislation by the new colonial legislature to provide for the administration of justice. They pointed out that:

> The judge holds every year ten courts of general gaol delivery in Melbourne and three on circuit at Geelong, . . . leaving the remote parts of the colony unvisited and rendering it necessary that prisoners should be brought in many instances a distance of two hundred or three hundred miles to either of these towns for trial. Four sittings of *nisi prius* of fourteen days each are held in Melbourne and three on circuit at Geelong of which the duration is uncertain. Besides this the judge sits weekly to dispose of proceedings in equity and other business. He is in addition liable to have applications, many of which are of great importance to the suitors, made to him almost daily in chambers and four times in the year he presides as Chairman of the Quarter Sessions. The extreme pressure of business of this multifarious nature not only entails on the judge, unaided as he is, excessive labour, but also much inconvenience on the suitors.[27]

They also criticized related delays and the necessary suspension of business in Melbourne while the sole judge was absent on circuit. Urgent writs, orders and injunctions simply could not be obtained, while "irreparable injury may be done to property, and fraudulent debtors have opportunities of effecting their escape from the colony".[28]

At last the qualms a'Beckett had entertained were allayed and he was appointed Chief Justice, the event being gazetted, provisionally, on 21 January 1852.[29] At the same time Redmond Barry, who since separation had held office as Solicitor-General, became first puisne judge.[30] The occupancy of the new positions took effect from 19 January. By July, Edward Eyre Williams was elevated to bring the bench to its full strength.[31] The new Chief Justice had been sworn in on 24 January 1852. The first effective sitting of the new court for public business took place, in Chambers, before a'Beckett alone on 2 February.[32]

"Our Independent Condition"

An earlier reviewer of a'Beckett's career pondered "what are we to make of ... the actual commission issued by La Trobe on 10 January 1853, appointing William a'Beckett, Esq., as Chief Justice of Victoria?".[33] The answer lies in the uncertainty generated by the Colonial Office's earlier foreshadowing that an imperial commission would issue to the new Chief Justice.[34] The appointment of a'Beckett, at first provisional, was confirmed in

August 1852 following the Colonial Office's assurances already mentioned.[35] Three weeks later a warrant was issued from "our Court at Osborne House, Isle of Wight" for the granting of a colonial, not an imperial, commission.[36] That flowed from the decision not to issue a Charter of Justice. Allowing for delays in communications, and the fact that La Trobe was preoccupied late in 1852 with tendering his resignation, it is not really surprising that the Chief Justice's commission did not issue until January 1853. In the meantime a'Beckett had augmented his new status as Chief Justice by publishing a small book with a prodigious title that may be reduced here to *The Magistrates' Manual for the Colony of Victoria*. It was a collation of statutory excerpts, with an insignificant commentary, drawing attention to the effects on the magistracy of the colonial adoption of *Jervis' Acts*.[37]

For a'Beckett, obtaining the Chief Justiceship was almost an anticlimax because his health robbed him of the capacity to discharge the duties of office to his best. He further struggled against the burden of the extraordinary times in which Melbourne was almost abandoned by its workforce, drawn away by the quest for gold. As Sir Archibald Michie recalled of the "fevered, drunken, delirious Pandemonium" of 1852: "The very police, the coachmen, the grooms, lawyers' clerks, ay, and even official men in large numbers, were off to the gold-fields; and even Sir William a'Beckett . . . (being at that time an invalid, and his coachman *non est*), had for some weeks to be wheeled to the court by his sons in a bath chair".[38]

Figuratively speaking, the first public steps of the new Chief Justice were faltering and misdirected, reflecting errors of diplomatic judgment on his part, exacerbated by a hostile newspaper press, especially the *Argus*, that watched relentlessly for any false move. It was soon made plain, for example, that a'Beckett was not applying uniform standards in the conduct of his court. He was not invariably the model of punctiliousness he expected from those in his court room. Thus, at his first chambers sitting, on 30 January 1852, a group of newly appointed magistrates attended to be sworn into office.[39] Inexplicably their commissions were not in the court, and a'Beckett had done nothing to ensure that they were. He declared abruptly that, without the commission instruments, which presumably he wished to inspect to confirm the legality of the appointments, he could administer no oaths. The proceedings were abandoned. The Chief Justice and his clerk must have shared some responsibility for failing to ensure that the necessary instruments were present. His intolerance of inadvertence or shortcomings in others will be mentioned shortly. His first substantive sitting, again in chambers, took place on 2 February when he disposed of two minor matters.[40]

Not until 10 February did a'Beckett make his first truly public appearance as Chief Justice, when he presided at the inaugural criminal sittings of the Supreme Court. He decided to use the occasion to settle two scores by delivering a "charge" to the jury. The panel of jurors then assembled comprised a petit jury. The convention was that a judge, in a charge, might draw the attention of a *grand* jury to matters within its power to correct – the state of public works, or the prevalence of particular crimes being typical instances. Two Sydney judges, Burton and Willis, for purposes of their own, had delivered charges to petit juries, there being then no grand jury in New South Wales. The consequences had been so inflammatory that prudence must have suggested that the precedent not be followed: a'Beckett himself, in February 1852, conceded that the practice was irregular.[41] But he could not resist adding to the sense of occasion of the first "Assize" sittings at Melbourne and Geelong.

The first score the Chief Justice sought to settle harked back to the consequences of *Marquis of Ailsa* v. *Watson* and his sense of frustration at having been stultified by the jurisdictional decisions of the Supreme Court in Sydney. Now he, and the Victorian court, were freed from those shackles, a result he found "gratifying". He declared to his numerous gallery that he deprecated the long continuance of the former Port Phillip court over which he had presided "under a name and form so repugnant to our independent condition". Justice, he declared jubilantly, "is no longer administered in one Colony by the Judge of a Court which belongs to *another*".[42]

That might have been harmless enough in itself, but the second score, to which he turned, was quite another matter. The criminal calendar for the inaugural sitting was "the heaviest ever held in Melbourne".[43] He was determined to alert the community to his conviction that the increase in crime was due almost entirely to the incipient gold rushes: a conviction that he simultaneously propounded as an anonymous pamphleteer. It was one thing for a Chief Justice to advance a contentious social theory in printed form under a pseudonym. It was quite another thing to use the judicial bench to seek to recruit the sympathy of jurors and a wider community to what were essentially personal, if well intentioned, views.

Taking such a course was the more reckless given the predictable response of the press. While the respective positions, judicial and journalistic, occupied extreme poles, it is clear that, on this occasion, the Chief Justice overreached himself and that the reaction of the newspapers, particularly the *Argus*, was reasonable and convincing.

The jury in this instance was treated to a discourse, of perhaps 30 minutes' duration, expressed in the effusive grandiloquence that passed for public oratory at that time. Taking great pride in his own literary attainments, a'Beckett embroidered his theme with many pompous embellishments that seem ludicrous to modern eyes, and were not spared criticism then. In essence, he declared that the quest for gold had introduced to Victoria a change "over the brightness of its prospects, which . . . seemed to destroy all the promise of its primal dawn". He deplored the spectacle of vast numbers of men leaving urban settlements to pursue their fortunes on the goldfields.

> The merchant saw his counting house suddenly deserted; the tradesman, his shop; the agriculturist, his farm; the squatter, his station; whilst offers contemptuously refused, or demands too exorbitant to be complied with, obliged many to abandon their vocation altogether, and, for a time at least, to resort to the very pursuit against whose seductions they were not wealthy or bold enough to bid.[44]

The jury could do nothing but listen in silence. The *Argus*, however, was less restrained. It declared itself to be "startled" by these remarks and, after two days' reflection, published its editorial disapproval, with the object of administering a "severe censure".[45]

"The more deeply we pondered it", announced the *Argus* concerning the charge, "the more dissatisfied we felt both with the sentiments it contains, and with the manner of expressing them". It found the style of the address highly objectionable and beneath the dignity of the occasion. It was "very like that of a boyish aspirant to literary fame or a junior member of a spouting club". Applying itself to the very words a'Beckett had used, it mocked a particular paragraph:

> in which fabled heroes, boy-Demigods, strangled serpents, nascent energies, primal dawns, ominous vibrations, electric wires, and more besides, are jumbled together in bewildering confusion, [which] is not even tolerable as a literary composition. No one reading this ridiculous flourish detached from the address, could suppose it to form a part of the charge of a Chief Justice, addressing a handful of sober, prosaic citizens, assembled to adjudicate on cases involving the temporal destiny of their fellow men.[46]

It assessed the charge as "meaningless bombast": the patience of the jury and others must have been tried severely in being obliged to sit through it. Having attacked a'Beckett's literary pretensions, the *Argus* turned with scorn to the substance of his remarks. It contended that the "cupidity" discerned by the Chief Justice in gold digging was unrealistic and unreasonable. Why was a gold seeker more avaricious than a merchant, a lawyer, or anyone else wanting money in exchange for work? The private sentiments of a'Beckett were, it thought, injudicious and calculated to aggravate rather than to relieve any evils that might exist. It concluded that social crises precipitated by the discovery of gold fields were beyond human foresight or human power to control. "We do not know", it declared contemptuously, "and we do not care, how far Chief Justice a'Beckett is answerable to pecuniary considerations, but we believe that we owe his presence less to any natural predilection for the employment, than to the seductions of a salary of fifteen hundred a year".[47]

Four days later, the *Argus* returned to the attack. It again dismissed the literary aspects of the charge – "the stiltedness of their style is harmless, and merely provokes ridicule".[48] But the substantive issues were not to be dismissed so lightly. The Chief Justice occupied a position of power and influence and had sought to use that authority to sway public affairs. The detachment expected of the judiciary should not, it thought, be compromised in such a way. His reflection, as a judge, on men who were merely miners was "unfair and ungenerous", and a wanton disparagement of the ordinary labouring man who sought to advance himself in life – availing himself of his chance and committing no crime. It was preposterous, the writer concluded, to characterize such men as having "ranged themselves against the society of which they form so material a part".

The Chief Justice conceded nothing and soon had an occasion to demonstrate the fact. On 19 February 1852 he arrived at Geelong to open, on the following day, the first circuit sittings of the new Supreme Court. He made "a sort of triumphal entry into Geelong", being received, as he put it, by a "highly respectable *cortège* of gentlemen ... on his way overland ... [who] escorted him into town".[49] At the opening of the court he addressed himself to another captive jury and reiterated his warnings of the grave threats to Victoria's social fabric that were generated by the prevailing mania for gold. He dismissed, as being "beneath notice", "one or two instances" in which his opinions had been challenged.

This time, however, his remarks were overshadowed by what followed. The entire sittings had to be adjourned *sine die* for procedural irregularity, and all the grand ceremony and lofty words were eclipsed by the realization that great carelessness had attended the convening of the circuit. On that very morning, the *Geelong Advertiser* published a broad hint that there appeared not to have been promulgated the necessary proclamation by the Governor authorizing the circuit.[50] Court officials, the Crown Law Officers, the Chief Justice and his clerk might all reasonably have been expected to have examined the *Advertiser's* suggestion and to have been prepared for any consequences.

On the contrary, as the last echoes of the Chief Justice's charge faded, and the first prisoner was placed in the dock for trial, there was such a flurry of activity at the Bar table, that the indictment could not be read. Attorney-General Stawell rose in embarrassment to propose that he and the Crown Solicitor confer with the Chief Justice in private chambers. Following that hasty conference, at which the *Advertiser's* forecasts were vindicated, Stawell moved that the sittings be suspended, as they were, and the jury was discharged. The whole empty ceremony had gone for nothing: a'Beckett's homily was forgotten in a mood of recrimination over a lapse in the very procedural strictness that a'Beckett expected of those involved in the business of the court. The press could not contain its glee. The *Advertiser* supposed that the Chief Justice did not trouble to read its columns:

> But it was cruel in the officers of the Court, or the friends of the Judge, not to have given him, before the form of opening had gone to so great a length, a hint of the existence of the grave doubt. . . A few minutes earlier intimation would have prevented the humiliating antithesis afforded by the opening ceremonies and the undignified conclusion.[51]

The stature of the Chief Justice, judicial and personal, was not enhanced by those two ceremonial sittings. The "charges" he delivered were so inappropriate that persistence with his fixation about gold placed him in a position as untenable as that of King Canute facing the incoming tide. Ordinary Victorians did not share a'Beckett's perceptions of the subject and were unimpressed by them. Gold was generally considered to be the foundation of colonial advancement and prosperity. The Chief Justice was completely out of touch with popular sentiment on the subject, and, in maintaining his views, he revealed a surprising want of acumen and discernment.

There was disapproval too of the way in which he had shrugged off two serious procedural lapses on the part of the court itself, while at once demanding the strictest accountability from those attending court, especially as lawyers or jurors. It was no excuse, he insisted, that the uncertain times and the dislocation they caused might render jurors late in arrival at court.[52] On the contrary, they were under a heightened obligation to allow for hindrances and ensure their own punctuality. No leniency would be allowed to defaulters. Likewise, no concessions would be permitted to jurors having to travel over long distances, on bad roads, or in poor weather. And, as for those seeking to be excused on the grounds of illness, medical certificates would not be accepted unless verified by affidavit.[53]

If he seemed hard on others, he was sometimes hard on himself. So exercised was he by the accumulation of court business that he was minded to forgo a public holiday appointed in July 1852 to celebrate the founding of the Colony. He felt that all involved should not spare a day that could be used to further the interests of justice. Court staff and litigants did not share his enthusiasm, but only after strenuous representations was he prevailed upon to change his mind on the very eve of the holiday.[54]

It was consonant with these strict notions of how business should be done that a'Beckett treated literally and inflexibly the established rules and practice of the court. As he remarked to the inaugural criminal sitting:

> I rejoice at the thought that I have never witnessed any symptoms of disrespect or contempt for them [the court's conventions], among the large portion of the colonists who have been in the habit of attending this court during the six years I have had the honour of presiding as its sole judge.[55]

That rejoicing was underwritten by severe sanctions the Chief Justice meted out to those not complying with the court's requirements and expectations.[56]

On the court's civil side there was more work to be done than three judges could well manage, many of the cases being complex and involving significant sums of money. Interlocutory hearings were shared around as the lists permitted – "one Judge dashes off the cases today, another puts them on tomorrow. . . So much for judicial consistency".[57] When the Chief Justice came to preside over, and deliver judgment at, a final trial, he found the task increasingly burdensome. Where once he had showed a zest in resolving legal problems, and had handed down stimulating and lucid decisions, circumstances had changed. His physical infirmities, the discordant state of society, and the poisoned barbs of the press, had blunted his ability to expound the law. He later admitted how much he had been wearied by "all the irksome brainwork" that the court's civil business demanded.

Thus, for example, in a much publicized libel case, *Whyte* v. *Young*, in March 1852, the jury were left in a state of confusion by a'Beckett's summing up. The action arose from a dispute about the boundaries of a run that had gone for determination to the Caveat Commissioner, before whom the plaintiff allegedly perjured himself. The defendant published a suggestion of the perjury and, on being sued for defamation, pleaded justification on the grounds of truth and public benefit. While warning the jury that the question was not one of title to land, the Chief Justice gave a disquisition on that very issue, concluding the "the more we begin to speculate upon and to analyse the evidence, the more do we see the difficulty of asserting that either plaintiff or defendant must have known when he was making a wrong assertion".[58]

That the jury had been anything but assisted by the Chief Justice's observations was attested by their prolonged failure to agree. After six hours, a three-fourths majority verdict was accepted and, even then, it was clear that the real issues had not been well understood. The judgment was to be for the plaintiff, with damages of one farthing.[59]

A further instance of a jury's being left in uncertainty by the evidence and the Chief Justice's exposition of it was *Khull* v. *Sheppard* in March 1852. It was another contest about the possession of a run. The summing up, declaring that "it was extremely difficult to define what powers were conferred by a squatting license", was not calculated to enlighten the jury. In this case a general verdict was given for the defendant but only after prolonged disagreement among the jurors.[60]

With his new judicial colleagues, a'Beckett carried a large burden of work on the criminal side of the court in 1852 and 1853. It must have been galling to the Chief Justice that, by the time Mr Justice Williams had been appointed to bring the Bench to its full strength in the winter of 1852, the *Argus* made it appear that a'Beckett had been virtually idle. The cause list in the Supreme Court had continued to expand, "still the business has been almost all disposed of", so it wrote, "by the assiduous attendance of Mr Justice Barry".[61] The new judge had indeed got through a vast amount of criminal work, but a'Beckett had been equally energetic. The press bestowed no praise on him for any good works, as, for example, when he lent towards recent English reforms that had rendered the crime of rape non-capital, and spared the life of a less serious offender, notwithstanding that colonial law still prescribed the death penalty.[62]

On the contrary, the *Argus* maintained a relentless pressure in exposing what it regarded (disingenuously) as shortcomings in the conduct of criminal trials by the Chief Justice. In June 1852, it rounded on a'Beckett with unbridled spleen, accusing him of encouraging juries to convict in criminal cases, of allowing unconscionable verdicts to stand uncorrected, and of demonstrating a judicial leaning towards severe punishment of criminals. "We believe", it declaimed,

> that the state of insecurity to life and property, which has grown up under the "firm and judicious" rule of one of the most incapable of men [a'Beckett], has so impressed the public mind with a sort of

> terror, and so impregnated it with notions of the necessity for making examples, that juries have been unconsciously guided by their fears, to the sacrifice of their judgments, and have found persons guilty upon very slight foundations, in a hope thereby to strike terror into others.[63]

There was no shred of evidence to support those assertions. The Chief Justice's inclination to clemency in criminal cases is well documented.[64] This time, it was the *Argus* that had overreached itself, having characterized the head of the judiciary falsely and unreasonably. It was as if that journal had determined to follow the lead of the *Sydney Monitor* that had so constantly, mercilessly, and for similar reasons of interest, hounded Sir James Dowling when a Judge and Chief Justice of the Supreme Court of New South Wales.[65] So stung was Victoria's Chief Justice by the undeserved reflections of the *Argus* that he determined to seek relief and separate himself from his tormentors by taking leave.

"I Forgot All the Irksome Brainwork"

By October, a'Beckett had solicited his leave, having reflected, no doubt, on the shabby treatment by the Colonial Office of the sick leave applications of Sir Francis Forbes and Sir James Dowling in New South Wales, by which their respective deaths had been hastened. His medical adviser, Dr Thomas, certified that the Chief Justice's paralytic condition was a "disease . . . affecting the nervous system", that had become increasingly aggravated within the doctor's observations extending over seven years. He recommended an immediate change of climate with total rest to the mind.[66]

The Chief Justice himself pointed out that no local medical man had been able to discover the cause of the derangement or to prescribe any effective remedy. The paralysis deprived him, not only of locomotion, but also of the sense of touch in his hands and feet, and his sense of taste was diminished.[67] In 1851, a specialist physician, visiting from India, had attributed the problem to Melbourne's climate. The Chief Justice wrote to the Governor that "want of pecuniary means alone prevented me from sooner following their advice; for I need hardly say that the allowance of half salary without other resources would not, if I had obtained it, have enabled me to take advantage of leave of absence".[68] The

Legislative Council was not unanimous in raising the Chief Justice's salary to £2500 in January 1853 and allowing leave on full pay.[69] J.P. Fawkner protested that "the salary had been increased on account of the expense of living in Melbourne, and now it appeared that the Chief Justice was going for two years to England, where it was not so expensive to live". Fawkner, however, was one of a small minority. The *Argus* could not contain its fury, given that, at that very moment, the other two judges were visiting neighbouring Colonies during the long summer vacation. "The estimates came on", declared the editorialist:

> Two thousand five hundred pounds are not thought too much by a public willing to have justice at any price, when the discovery is made that the place can do very well without any judges at all. Like roguish school-boys watching the master's eye before the expected, yet doubtful, holiday is granted: the scarlet-robed sages ply their oars with, oh! what seeming attention. No sooner have the Estimates passed, when skip – off goes one to Van Diemen's Land, and another to Sydney, whilst the third bundles up his traps and prepares for a short excursion of sixteen thousand miles for *two* years. Meanwhile a heavy criminal calendar for the month is postponed. . . We believe this to be a job of such dimensions as would not – could not be perpetrated elsewhere.[70]

La Trobe felt much embarrassment in acceding to a'Beckett's request for leave which had come at a most awkward time. Even though the Lieutenant-Governor could see no hope of filling effectively the temporary vacancy, and a'Beckett himself had had no success in finding a *locum tenens*, La Trobe "judged it proper to concede leave of absence".[71] New South Wales barristers, so a'Beckett had pointed out, were not interested in taking interim positions in Victoria, especially given "the social and domestic discomforts of locating in a town like this, [and] the enormous expense at which alone, if at all, a household could be established by a newcomer".[72] One leader of the Sydney Bar, John Bayly Darvall, did visit Melbourne to consider accepting the appointment but, there being no hotel accommodation apart from "a comfortable shake-down on the top of a taproom table between two lucky diggers", he left straightway the day after arriving.[73]

Chief Justice a'Beckett sailed from Melbourne, in the *Northumberland*, on 4 February 1853.[74] Before departing he had received, in "the large dining-room" at the home of his brother

Thomas, "a deputation of gentlemen, consisting of nearly the whole of the legal profession", albeit only the solicitors' branch, who presented an address, read by Crown Solicitor Gurner. The document conveyed "our expression of respect and esteem for your high legal attainments, your conscientious industry . . . and your kind and courteous bearing to ourselves on all occasions". It acknowledged the "efficient and satisfactory manner" in which a'Beckett had conducted the court since arriving as Resident Judge. His Honour, "with much emotion", declared that he would "ever recur to the testimony of your approbation with feelings of pleasure and pride". He vowed, presciently, that he would treasure it as a "vindication" if his judicial character "should be made henceforth the subject of calumny or aspersion". He valued it more highly than "a burst of huzzas at any after-dinner demonstration".[75] At last, there was something to show, in the public scales, that would balance the venom of the *Argus*.

Before leaving for England, a'Beckett had the satisfaction of receiving a knighthood. The *Argus* broke the news in a sour humour, criticizing what it regarded as the "idle trappings" of the title and the "inordinate vanity of the recipient".[76] Knighthood was a customary recognition of Chief Justices of superior colonial courts, though, more often than not, attaining it required supplication. Sir William's means to that end cast some light on his cool relationship with La Trobe. It has sometimes been said that, in response to a general Colonial Office inquiry about the appropriateness of awarding honours, La Trobe advised against them, but proposed that an exception be made in a'Beckett's case.[77] In fact, La Trobe's opposition to colonial honours was absolute. He wrote, confidentially, to the Secretary of State, in August 1852, that, "however judicious the proposed measure may be held to be in the abstract and however satisfactorily it may be carried into effect in a few years' time, its application to this Colony may be considered a little premature and better deferred for the present".[78] The Colonial Office thought that the Lieutenant-Governor should have "explained himself a little more fully in a confidential despatch"[79] and was, accordingly, receptive to an application, made on a'Beckett's behalf, by his barrister brother Gilbert, an influential political journalist and foundation member of the staff of London *Punch*.[80]

La Trobe was vexed that Sir William had bypassed the normal channel of communicating with the Colonial Office through him, and had forestalled his objections to colonial honours. As La Trobe wrote to Deas Thomson, Colonial Secretary in New South Wales:

> a'Beckett is going home on leave having literally *punched* the honour of a knighthood out of Sir J. Pakington. Without making known his scheme to me he employed his brother *Mr Gilbert a'Beckett* as his agent - and the assumption and pertness with which he went to work is highly amusing.[81]

The *bon mot* hides a sense of antipathy, probably extending to jealousy, felt by La Trobe towards a'Beckett. Although they had constantly to work together on official matters, their association seems never to have advanced beyond that of reserved formality. The Chief Justice's visits to Government House, even on social occasions, were limited, and the occasions themselves were impersonal to the point of frostiness. One published biography of La Trobe makes only a single reference to a'Beckett, and that concerning their joint attendance at a public ceremony.[82]

La Trobe isolated himself considerably from the benefit of legal advice in the conduct of his administration. He was lofty enough to consider his own opinion superior to those of others about him qualified to give counsel. He despised Croke, not unreasonably, and considered him incompetent.[83] On the other hand, while normally shunning the Chief Justice, he seemed content to make use of a'Beckett's knowledge of protocol and drafting ability when the need arose. For instance, in 1847, Pohlman wrote in his diary, "remained in town late expecting to receive for signature the address of condolence to the Governor [on the death in a coach accident of Lady Mary FitzRoy] which I heard the Judge having written had taken to Mr La Trobe in order that it might be sent round for the purpose".[84]

The Chief Justice's travels in which he was, as he put it, "out of harness", interrupt the thread of his judicial career and will be considered later. In his absence, gossip was quickly generated that he would return much earlier than planned, as the real purpose of taking leave was to solicit an "exchange" of his Victorian position for an County Court Judgeship in England, which proposal had been rejected there. So pressing were the rumours that Thomas a'Beckett wrote to the press to deny every element of them.[85] The

Chief Justice did not abbreviate his leave.[86] When he returned to Melbourne after two years, in January 1855, his mind might have been refreshed, but his health was not restored. As he wrote of one section of his travels in Italy:

> [I] forgot for the time all the irksome brainwork and heartfelt anxieties of gone-by years in distant climes . . . [and composed] a prayer that I might go back to that distant clime and irksome brainwork . . . a better if not a haler man.[87]

4

Eureka and Beyond

Almost immediately, on resuming his place at the head of the Bench, it was obvious that the Chief Justice laboured under great physical indisposition. At a hearing on the criminal side, on 20 January 1855, it was reported that, "the court resumed its sittings at ten o'clock this morning, but broke up at an early hour, his Honor [a'Beckett] remarking that the close duties of the week, and the late sittings of the day before, had greatly fatigued him".[1] In the following month he was too unwell to be able to attend one of his more compelling extra-judicial commitments, the annual meeting of the Liquor Law League. He complained that "since his return to the Colony he had not felt the climate suit him so well as before".[2] And he protested that an array of medical advisers, English and colonial, had decreed such a curtailment of his public appearances that he was obliged to withdraw attendance at many activities he supported.[3]

Nevertheless he threw himself vigorously into the work of the court, and the large number of cases he disposed of, together with the volume of intricate judgments he delivered at that period, demonstrate that he had not lost his touch as a judicial lawyer of considerable ability. Paradoxically, many of those judgments demonstrate also an increase in commercial litigation that reflected the wealth and expansion brought to the Colony by the goldfields. As the *Victoria Law Times* observed, in 1857:

> Returning to us refreshed, but still uncured, and resuming his official labours, [the Chief Justice] has, on the whole, taken his seat so punctually, and presided with such a brave heart and persevering mind, as often to have excited admiration and the warmest sympathy.[4]

The Chief Justice needed all the encouragement that might go his way. His return to the Bench, and the remainder of his service on it, came to be dominated by two immense causes - the Eureka Trials and the case of George Dunmore Lang, which will be examined shortly. Much criticism was applied to a'Beckett for his part in those proceedings, a good deal of which, it is here suggested, was ill founded.

"Not the Place to Discuss a Question of Politics"

The essential facts of an uprising of miners at Ballarat, in angry response to the government's officious efforts to extract from them substantial licence fees for their gold seeking, and the ensuing "Eureka Stockade" and "State Trials", are widely known and will not be repeated here.[5] Few of the participants emerged from the proceedings with credit. In particular, Lieutenant-Governor Hotham (much despised by the miners generally, as representing a parsimonious and remote imperial power) exacerbated the conflict by his lack of tact and his proclamation of martial law.[6]

In political terms, "Eureka" has become enchanted ground: seen by many as the very source of Australian aspirations to nationhood, to independence founded on equality, and to resistance of overbearing authority. Any doubter of that creed is liable to be branded as a heretic and discredited. It is difficult, however, to perceive in Australia's equivalent to the "Boston Tea Party" much virtue in an *armed* uprising against a constitutional government. Such a course would not be tolerated now, and many Victorians thought it intolerable then.

This study will not, however, trespass far upon the enchanted ground, as the present concern is with legal, not political, issues. The starting point will be a prelude that began in a gathering on Bakery Hill at Ballarat on 29 November 1854. That was the very day before the dramatic events of the Stockade. The legal consequences of the gathering have been all but ignored by earlier writers who have been preoccupied with the "State Trials". In assessing the stature of Sir William a'Beckett, those consequences cannot be overlooked. That the gathering was neither orderly nor conciliatory was remarked upon by Professor Clark in these terms: "A digger tried to remind them that as all were British, they should use constitutional means to redress their grievances. He was shoved off the platform and only saved by the chairman from being torn to pieces".[7] These were commonly called "the Ballarat Riots" at the time, and they will be so described here to distinguish them from the "State Trials".

In the Supreme Court, in January 1855, six men, Goddard, Chapman, Ewing (or Ewins), McIntyre, Bryant (or Brian) and Campbell were put on trial, before the Chief Justice and a jury, on charges of conspiracy to excite contempt of the government, riot, assault and unlawful assembly. It was alleged that placards were displayed at the meeting to incite lawlessness, that "very strong language was used" and that many gold licences were burnt in public.[8] Solicitor-General Molesworth, as prosecutor, fairly pointed out that the trial was limited to the legal consequences of any acts proved, and was not concerned with the policy of gold licences.

> [He] thought a court of justice was not the place to discuss a question of politics, as to whether gold-diggers should or should not be made to pay a tax for the use of the lands where they discovered their treasures; this would be most unbecoming, either in himself or the jury.[9]

After much testimony had been received, Michie, for the defence, submitted that there was no evidence of conspiracy to go to the jury, and the Chief Justice replied, "No, not the slightest". There was, however, material enough to be put to the jury on other counts, though a'Beckett declared that he considered it to be insubstantial, and that only two of the accused men could possibly be implicated by it.[10]

His ensuing address demonstrated that a'Beckett was anything but attached to a preconceived point of view about gold-diggers for the purposes of these trials. He made it clear to the jury that most of the counts could not be sustained by the evidence. The only possible offence, implicating all, was unlawful assembly: and there, "the facts had been justly laid down by the counsel . . .; but the wrong conclusions had been drawn therefrom". The Bakery Hill gathering had been at liberty to canvass grievances "in the most unmeasured terms short of sedition", and no evidence had been adduced that the meeting was assembled for any unlawful purpose. It was not sufficient for the Crown to show that individuals formed part of an agitated crowd to attract the conclusion that there had been a riotous assembly. So advised, the jury needed only three minutes to reach a verdict that all of those charged were not guilty.

One may contrast the silence of the contemporary press and later commentators concerning these proceedings with the extravagant denunciations of the Chief Justice that followed the ensuing "State Trials", mentioned below. Nothing in this preliminary case suggested the slightest overbearing of the jury by the Chief Justice or the display by him of any preconception. He exemplified moderation. No-one cavilled at his judicial demeanour or maintained that he had been irritable. The only hint of the pressure that such an important case must have created came just before the charge to the jury, when the court officers spontaneously cried "silence", "upon which his Honor said, that as the court was perfectly quiet, he did not see any necessity for their creating an uproar by crying 'silence' ".[11]

"Any Felon Might Express Contrition"

It might have been supposed that the Executive Government, instructed by the outcome of the Ballarat Riots case, would have reconsidered its position. But Hotham, with the egregiously defective advice of Attorney-General Stawell,[12] resolved to raise the stakes. The proposal by the Gold Fields Commission, that there be a general amnesty, was rejected.[13] Thirteen prisoners, taken into custody at Eureka, were put on trial for high treason. It was incautious for the Attorney-General to attempt to make a case for such an extreme offence that was so out of keeping with colonial circumstances. It sought to apply to a very different antipodean society an essentially feudal notion in which the concept of a crime against "the state" could not be imagined.[14] Moreover, it stood with no apparent precedent in Australia, the well known "Rum Rebellion" under Governor Bligh in New South Wales having been disposed of as a military matter before a court martial on charges of mutiny.[15] Blackstone observed of treason that, "As this is the highest civil crime ... any man can possibly commit, it ought therefore to be the most precisely ascertained".[16] Accordingly, the information, at the Eureka trials followed precisely the terms of the then governing statute 25 *Edw.* III *stat* 5, *c.* 2 (1351).

Stawell, as a lawyer in politics, ought better to have sensed the state of popular opinion. It was so fixed against the Lieutenant-Governor that it flowed over into the jury box, ensuring verdicts of acquittal that were as much an indictment of Hotham as they were an exoneration of the supposed traitors. Stawell, taken aback, was obliged to defer the remaining cases for trial before another judge and a new jury.[17] The first treason trials, and some preliminary proceedings, heard before the Chief Justice, had been occasions of high drama, with the court house filled, and "thousands were observed waiting outside, vainly endeavouring to gain admittance" who "vociferously cheered" on seeing the prisoners led to and from the court.[18]

The most unlucky participant, who did not share the public sympathy shown for the others, was Henry Seekamp, editor of the *Ballaarat Times*, who was tried for sedition and found guilty, but recommended to mercy, and released from prison after only three months.[19] He had pleaded that an allegedly offensive publication in the *Times* had occurred without his knowledge or consent while he was absent from Ballarat.[20] One of the authors of the publication was said to be a son of the Revd Dr J.D. Lang, who had recently been at the centre of another *cause célèbre*.[21] In Seekamp's case, at least, a'Beckett was spared the pressure and party-feeling that attended the other treason trials. The *Argus* reported: "During the reading of the indictment all the court were convulsed with laughter - not forgetting His Honor the learned judge. The provocative to this mirth was the grandiloquent and over sublime phraseology in which the alleged seditious language was couched".[22] But there was no mirth when the other trials began. As H.G. Turner wrote of those proceedings, with no pretence of objectivity:

> It was unfortunate for the Crown that the first case was that of an American Negro, named Joseph. The presiding judge was Sir William a'Beckett, an upright, but very irritable occupant of the Bench. The prosecution was conducted by the Attorney-General, William Foster Stawell. . . The cold forensic knowledge of the Attorney-general, a man utterly destitute of the sense of humour, was no match for the scathing ridicule and biting sarcasm of the witty Aspinall [junior for the defence], who had the jury with him from the moment he began to speak.[23]

There was good reason for a'Beckett to have felt irritable on that occasion. Challenges to jurors occupied several hours, taking advantage of the special procedure in treason trials that permitted 35 peremptory challenges, instead of 20 allowed in the case of felony. In the result, according to the press, "the course of justice had almost the character of a farce".[24]

The Chief Justice, being well aware of community sentiment, was probably not much surprised by the speedy acquittal of Joseph, even though he had summed up "as the saying is 'dead against the prisoner' ". Moreover,

> The facts took place in the presence of hundreds: the counsel for the prisoner called no witnesses: the points at issue were supported by unquestionable testimony, no one had or could have the smallest doubt - and the prisoner was acquitted; not because he was not guilty in the legal sense, but because the jury did not think proper to convict him.[25]

In a curious twist, a'Beckett found himself placed in a position like that of Chief Justice Dowling at the "Myall Creek Massacre" trials, in Sydney in 1838.[26]

On the acquittal of Joseph, there had been spontaneous cheering in the courtroom, accompanied by "a most uproarious round of applause, [those in the galleries] clapping their hands and stamping their feet".[27] The Chief Justice, in a testy humour, declared that the demonstration was "one of the most disgraceful things he had ever seen in a Court of Justice" especially as it suggested a "kind of sinister intimidation of the jury".[28] He caused two of the ringleaders to be seized and committed to prison for contempt in the face of the court. That was on a Friday. On the following Monday, one of the malefactors, John Keogh, presented "a humble petition . . . couched in humiliating language . . . [and expressing] heartfelt contrition". The Chief Justice was unmoved. Contrition induced by punishment, he said, formed no rational basis for pardon: "On the same plan housebreakers, horse stealers or any felon might express contrition when punishment overtook them". These examples had been made by way of warning: on the occurrence of similar contempt more condign punishment should be expected.[29]

There followed the trial of John Manning, again for treason, in having "levied war against Her Majesty" and in having conspired to levy such war. Stawell prosecuted and was at pains to explain that the charge did not relate to Queen Victoria personally, it was about "an insurrection to induce the Government to change its measures, and by force to get the repeal of a particular law". That, in his view, constituted treason, and "the state of society was such that he was forced to it".[30] There was less excitement on this occasion than at Joseph's trial, though there was an anticlimax when the foreman of the jury forgot his lines:

> The Associate asked... Is the prisoner at the bar Guilty or Not Guilty?
> Foreman, with a sort of stammer: Guilty!
> Two or three jurors: What, what!
> Foreman: Oh! I meant *Not* Guilty.[31]

The announcement "caused a very agreeable sensation in Court", except, no doubt, at the side of the Bar table occupied by the Attorney-General, who had been severely rebuffed.

The trial of Joseph dominated editorial opinion in the colonial press for some days. In New South Wales, the *Sydney Morning Herald* declared that reasonable people should not have been deceived by an artful defence. The facts were, it said, that the prisoners had fired on the Queen's troops by preconceived design. The failure to secure a conviction reflected poorly, thought the *Herald*, on the jury system in Melbourne, and showed up, as "craven", jurymen who acted in fear of the consequences to them should they give a decision contrary to that which "the galleries of the court indicate ... they expect". It inferred that the judge's conduct of the trial lacked moral courage, especially in his having remained silent when, in the editorialist's view, he should, on the one hand, have pointed out the fallacies of counsel's arguments and, on the other hand, have restrained "the mob" from "exhibit[ing] unmistakeably what they think". Weakness, like this, on the part of judge and jury would, the *Herald* conceived, undermine the entire working of government and of law and order.[32]

In Victoria, criticisms of a'Beckett came from different perspectives. The *Melbourne Morning Herald* was disposed to side with the Chief Justice – "no more upright or merciful magistrate than Sir William a'Beckett ever graced the judicial bench".[33] It thought the result of the trial predictable because the crime charged was too extreme. The jury, it contended, "doubtless thought most of these prisoners guilty of something, but not High Treason". It parted company, however, from that part of the Chief Justice's address which declared that: "The law of this colony was more favourable to popular freedom than the law of England in securing the liberty of the people. We were ahead of it". The *Melbourne Herald* was convinced that the Chief Justice had no practical knowledge of the goldfields, where the state of society was "un-English, and unwarranted by British precedents . . . we really are at a loss to see by what perversion of language it can be contended with any degree of plausibility, that the diggers as a class, are directly cared for by the British Constitution at all".[34]

The *Argus* was indignant that the Chief Justice (in fact, very properly) not only had suppressed publication of the evidence before completion of the trial, but also had promised that transgressors would be visited with proceedings for contempt. "The publicity of all legal proceedings", said the *Argus* grandly, "is the guarantee to society that they are fairly conducted. The purity of the bench, the vigilance of the bar, and the fidelity of the jury are not enough". Otherwise, the *Argus* was content to direct its censures to Stawell.[35]

The most personal attack on the Chief Justice, the effects of which have long endured, came from the *Age*. It deplored his charge to the jury in Joseph's case as being one-sided, as having "denounced" all the prisoners, and as having sought to "hunt" them down. It declared that "His Honor was labouring under chronic irritability and charged the jury with the judicial bayonet, as if bent on a capture". On that view, "It was high time for Melbourne juries to assume an independent position, and to step in between the people and their oppressors"[36] – the exact opposite of the contentions of the *Sydney Morning Herald*. Of the Manning trial, the *Age* presumed to write:

> We must not omit to congratulate Sir William a'Beckett on his amended tone. Though it was still evident that his sympathies were with the prosecution, he maintained something of the dignity and impartiality becoming the bench, and had evidently profited by the just strictures passed on his previous deportment.[37]

Other contemporary prints do not corroborate those views: they were naked hyperbole. But, having been adopted by Turner and others, to add colour to later accounts of the occasion, they have lived on to the very great prejudice of a'Beckett's reputation. They are, however, minor reflections when weighed against relatively recent legal criticisms of the Chief Justice that must now be examined with care.

"Duress is a Matter of Defence"

Under the influence of the aspersions of the *Age*, the summing up by the Chief Justice, in Joseph's trial, has been noticed with disparagement. But, when read, today, in the absence of the tensions of the moment, it appears as a reasoned and well balanced advice, apart from its sanctimonious peroration which urged the jury to accept divine guidance. That has been described as "theological intimidation",[38] which, quite clearly, it was not when taken in its context. It came as a reminder to the jurors of their duty under oath, and as an addendum to the Chief Justice's only reference to the great public excitement attracted by the case. He said:

> He would now leave the question to the jury and he would entreat of them to disregard whatever expectations may have been formed by any man or any body of men inside or outside the Court, as to what verdict they would give.[39]

Then came the invocation of "Him on whose gospel they had sworn to give a true verdict", which the *Age* condemned as "conceived in the worst possible taste, and . . . very much like the fag end of a prosy Unitarian sermon".[40] The *Age* might have mentioned also that the practice of appealing to religious sentiment was common among colonial judges and was in harmony with the usages of the times. Unlike the rest of the Chief Justice's charge, this entreaty was couched in the exaggerated language he employed on such occasions. Suffice it to say that, in *R.* v. *Joseph*, it did not sway the jury to accept the Crown's case.

Treating it as axiomatic that Attorney-General Stawell had grossly misjudged public opinion in his decision to proceed by way of charges of treason, there is no ground for taking an extra step and associating the Chief Justice with that misjudgment. The prosecutor, not the judge, necessarily defined the course of the trial. Sir William a'Beckett had to take the information as he found it. There was no merit, so he instructed the jury, in a defence argument that the proceedings were unconstitutional or "repugnant to the spirit and law" of England – or of Victoria. The counts were founded literally on the statute of Edward III, and authorities (including passages from Sir Michael Foster's, *Report of Commission for Trial of Rebels in 1746*) constrained him to advise that there was an arguable case of levying war – "the gravamen of the whole information". "If", he said, "they [the jury] found the men, of whom the prisoner was one, doing certain acts, fighting with the Queen's troops, and setting all law and order at defiance, then that was levying war".[41] As the *Argus* reported his words, he told the jury that,

> If they found that [the diggers] had waged war against the Queen's troops, that they had set the law at defiance, that they had disturbed the peace of the Queen's subjects, then they might determine that such conduct was treasonable.[42]

In those directions, there was no overbearing of the jury or undue influence of their decision. The Chief Justice made allowance for the customs of the gold fields where many men carried arms. The mere fact of being seen with arms would not, he said, support a finding against the prisoner. Nor would the mere fact of there being a display of the "Eureka" flag. But there was evidence of the men, including Joseph, being "drilled" as if a military contingent, of ringleaders exhorting them "Now was the time to take the law into their own hands", and that "Lawler [*scil.* Peter Lalor] knelt down and swore that they would all fight for and defend each other; and the assemblage cried amen".[43]

It is surprising and disappointing that the assessments of two retired judges from Victoria, relying on supposedly legal grounds that seem superficial, have criticized a'Beckett's management of the trial. Thus Professor Graham L. Fricke, Q.C., (a former County Court Judge) has written that a'Beckett's charge was delivered "in somewhat partisan and tendentious terms", "had the effect of reversing the onus of proof" and "neglected to point out that at that time an accused person was not permitted to give evidence".[44] Sir Arthur Dean (a former Supreme Court Judge) had earlier declared *ex cathedra* that a'Beckett had altered the onus of proof in a manner that was "particularly unjust". Sir Arthur, at least, conceded that "in accordance with the law books at that time it was for the accused to satisfy the jury of his innocence once the Crown proved facts inculpating him".[45] How else, it might be asked, is a judge to conduct highly controversial criminal proceedings than in accordance with the "law books" (including statutes and precedent authority) of the time? Such a forum, in such circumstances, is not one for bold judicial spirits to undertake brave experiments in law reform, or to prophesy what views might be taken of current law in later centuries. Perceiving old laws through modern eyes can be a deceptive course if those laws are expected to have been applied, in their own day, with the same "enlightenment" revealed to later generations.

Sir William a'Beckett was a master of procedural law. It would do much less than justice to his professional stature to suppose that he acted, in Joseph's case, in ignorance or disregard of the law, (albeit very esoteric law), that related to treason in the mid nineteenth century. The passage of his address to the jury, that has attracted modern censure, was reported thus:

> Putting all the circumstances together, could they for a moment affirm that [Joseph] had been in the stockade merely as an innocent spectator? Were that the truth, it would have been easy, it would lie with him to prove that such was the case. If he could have sworn that he was there on compulsion, and that he had given himself up, saying, "I am here by restraint, and I surrender", there would have been some grounds for such a belief, but there was no evidence to show anything of the kind.[46]

Another report then continued, "although it was with the Crown to show the character of the acts, *yet when they have proved that in the way they have done here,* it rests with the prisoner to show that he was not there with this same object as the rest".[47] That statement was made in circumstances where H.S. Chapman, the leading defence counsel, had resolved upon a potentially risky strategy of calling no witnesses and advising Joseph not to exercise the right to make a statement, ordinarily permitted in treason trials, after his counsel had spoken. The latter procedure was well-established[48] – there was no "neglect" by the Chief Justice to comment on the inability of an accused person to give evidence for himself in a criminal trial. That was then the law: it needed no restatement.

The effect of a'Beckett's remarks to the jury was that the Crown had discharged the onus of proof falling to it. On that basis alone the jury might find against the prisoner. But there could have been another path of escape which Chapman had declined to use. Had the defence of duress been raised, even though the case was one of treason, the court would have entertained it. English law on that point has been ambivalent over the years,[49] but the trial of Joseph establishes that, in Victoria in 1855, duress could have been a defence to a charge of treason. That being so, the Chief Justice did not, as the law then stood, *reverse* the onus of proof. It was for the Crown, as mentioned in the passage italicized above, to prove the character of the acts. Once that was done, had duress been raised, "duress is a matter of defence and the onus of proving it is on the accused".[50]

Professor Fricke, Q.C., declares the Eureka trials and the acquittals (of all but Seekamp) to redound to the credit of "stalwart juries who refused to be intimidated by a government – supported by the judiciary – intent upon securing convictions".[51] It strains the surviving written evidence, and all credibility, to suggest that a'Beckett, and Mr Justice Barry in the remaining trials, forswore their judicial oaths to accommodate the government. The Chief Justice, in the Ballarat Riots trial, had manifested the plainest impartiality. Only by a contorted reading of his charge in *R. v. Joseph* can it be contended that he there displayed prejudice or even irritability. The thesis of Professor Fricke, that the Eureka juries revealed the capacity of the jury, as an institution, to rise above the executive government and the judiciary, represents, surely, a two-edged sword. It might equally be said that public opinion at the time was so set against the concept of treason, that (given the large number of challenges allowed in treason trials) no jury with an independent mind could conceivably have been impanelled. Sir William a'Beckett had rightly perceived the influence of "expectations", formed by the community, on how the jury should act.

Apart from the above quoted passages about the burden of proof (which, it is submitted, have been misconstrued), and some observations on "digger hunting" and military "spies" who infiltrated the diggers – which were extraneous to the issues for trial, not one sentence from the Chief Justice's charge is quoted to support the interpretation that he was partisan, tendentious, unjust or otherwise unreasonable. It is not obvious, on reading any report of them, that his observations are open to that construction. Nor is it patently clear, in the light of the uncontradicted Crown evidence before the court, how any judge, as the law then stood, could have summed up in terms significantly different from those used by a'Beckett. The better view is that, in extraordinarily difficult circumstances, a'Beckett comported himself with high judicial propriety and with exactness and fairness to the extent that the law then allowed.

Nothing survives to reveal a'Beckett's private views about these trials. It was clear that, in public, he was nettled by some tactics used for the defence, and particularly by the provocative style of advocacy employed by B.C. Aspinall, junior counsel in Joseph's trial.[52] The Chief Justice was also disquieted by the reaction of the gallery and by the drift of public opinion that so dominated the proceedings. In the latter respect, according to the Chief Justice's son W.A.C. a'Beckett, it had become plain for all to see that Victoria was on the path to a new order in which Sir William could not feel comfortable:

> The prisoners were tried for high treason before my father, and he was consequently very unpopular with the new democratic class that was springing up in the colony; but his views were thoroughly tory and conservative and unfit for the new state of things brought about by the "Diggings", which he always deplored as a calamity to the country.[53]

That was a frank assessment, but it conceals the unenviable position of a judge in litigation that involves social and political issues liable to inflame fervent passions. It was not for the Chief Justice to mould his office to attract popularity. He occupied that office to uphold the law. At whatever cost to his reputation, Sir William did his duty.

"A Perfect Outrage Upon Justice"

The Lang case preceded the Eureka trials and was no less burdensome to the Chief Justice. It is convenient now to consider it out of sequence. George Dunmore Lang, eldest son of the controversial Presbyterian cleric Dr John Dunmore Lang, M.L.C.,[54] was sentenced by the Chief Justice, after trial by jury, to imprisonment with hard labour. George Lang had been manager of the gold-buying agency to the Bank of New South Wales at Ballarat. He and the bank's branch accountant, Frederick Lee Drake, were convicted of embezzling a substantial sum. While Dr Serle states that "the suspicion has remained down the years that the charge was got up . . . to discredit the father",[55] later studies suggest an even higher suspicion that the defalcations were so great as to have demanded independent scrutiny.[56] Nevertheless, the Revd Dr Lang, feeling personally affronted, intervened on his son's behalf with the incautious enthusiasm and tenacity that were typical of him. As R.F. Holder put it, Lang senior campaigned "by slaying and slandering every philistine who got in the way".[57] These were, Lang insisted, "matters of public concernment" in which he had "a clear call from God to interfere".[58] That call suggested to him that he write a long letter to the Melbourne *Argus* to condemn the court proceedings and the presiding judge. Part of the letter, as published, read:

> The circumstance that has excited equal astonishment and indignation on the part of intelligent and disinterested persons in Sydney, as it has also done very generally in [Victoria], is the conduct of the Chief Justice in the case. That functionary appears to have acted throughout as if he had held a brief for the prosecution, and had been determined to bring the whole weight and influence of the bench, in addition to that of the bank, against the prisoners, - ignoring every circumstance that told in their favour, exaggerating everything that seemed to tell against them, outraging the common sense of the community by his *dicta* and observations on the occasion, and, I will not hesitate to add, virtually compromising the bench by identifying it with the prosecution.[59]

He continued thus, heaping invective upon invective, as he traced a'Beckett's colonial connexions to the class of lawyers "hostile to popular freedom and the rights of men" and asserted that a'Beckett's "judicial shafts" were really directed to the reverend gentleman himself because of his known advocacy of popular causes. The fountain of justice, he wrote, had been hopelessly polluted by the misdeeds of this "colonial Judge Jeffreys on the bench". Lang concluded that, "if it shall be your opinion that Sir William a'Beckett has compromised his own character, and that of the bench over which he presides, in the late trial, he will neither have been the first nor the only Australian Chief Justice who has done so, even within my own personal experience and observation".[60]

While "certain kind friends" pressed the complainant to place his son's case before the Executive, Lang was much too wily to transact that kind of business in his own name. He did the devilling and prevailed upon his kind friends - not least William Kerr, erstwhile editor of the *Argus* and avowed a'Beckett hater - to be seen to be the moving parties. Soon there was a public meeting, followed by a flood of petitions, memorials and other representations supporting review of the convictions. Many of the submissions annexed letters from supposedly interested persons, all of whom, by the merest of coincidences, happened spontaneously to write to Dr Lang. There were many weighty applications, one from the Town Council of Geelong to the effect that the venue for the trial had been laid wrongly in Melbourne and should have been at Ballarat,[61] while every non-lawyer supplicant professed a view on the law at odds with that propounded by the Chief Justice.

Disconcerted by the latter reflections, a'Beckett surprisingly yielded to a request from the Acting Governor that he review and comment on the various documents received by the Executive. The Chief Justice was ill-advised to have done so. He was *functus officio,* unless to assist the Executive Council in considering questions of pardon or parole of the persons convicted. By giving a report, which he did at considerable length and in great detail, he proceeded, as it were, to deliver a discrete judgment upon the trial and to re-open discussion of it. He said that he acted thus "considering the strong language in which the justice of the verdict and the fairness of the trial have been impugned".[62] In essence, he dismissed all of the representations as failing to comprehend the law as to embezzlement, and he thought the grounds adduced in support of pardon or clemency were "totally fallacious and untenable, both in reference to the law and facts upon which their conviction took place".[63]

To keep the matter on the boil, J.D. Lang composed and published another of his many pamphlets on public issues. This one he called *The Convicts' Bank*.[64] In it, as well as defaming other parties, including the proprietors of the Bank of New South Wales - for which he was ultimately found guilty of criminal libel and sentenced to six months' imprisonment - he returned to his attack on a'Beckett. He described the trial of his son as "a perfect outrage upon justice and common sense", in which the contribution of the Chief Justice had been "flippant and heartless" to an unseemly degree. "In short", he concluded, "his Honor's justice in this case was not British but Chinese justice".[65]

Like the Eureka trials, the result of these proceedings was perverse. Setting an undesirable precedent, (nevertheless followed in even greater *causes célèbres* in Australian legal history), the Victorian Executive, advised by the legislature, constituted itself a virtual court of appeal and overruled the Chief Justice's considered opinion on the jury's convictions, in the light of a report from a Select Committee of the Legislative Assembly. In recommending clemency for the prisoners, that committee was pleased to pronounce that the Chief Justice had excluded evidence – particularly character evidence – which, if before the jury, would have tended to demonstrate that the accused were innocent. That "ruling", on a matter of law, confounded the separation of powers between the legislature and the judiciary, and inappropriately interfered with the administration of justice. Nevertheless, at the cost of suffering imprisonment himself, Dr Lang had proclaimed the acceptable year of the Lord and seen his son and Drake released from custody in 1857.

While it has been suggested that a'Beckett himself initiated a prosecution of J.D. Lang for libel amounting to contempt, the initiative was that of Stawell as Attorney-General.[66] He filed an *ex officio* information against Lang "for having, as a wicked and evil disposed person, . . . written and caused to be published a wicked and scandalous libel in the *Argus* newspaper, reflecting on the administration of justice, and intending to bring the same into contempt; by implying that Sir William a'Beckett had improperly used his influence, as a judge" to procure a conviction against G.D. Lang and Drake.[67] The proceedings were heard before Mr Justice Barry and a jury. Dr Lang appeared in person to conduct his defence, and did so to devastating effect, appealing to the jury's sympathy in recognizing his standing as the parent of a son of allegedly unblemished character who had been greatly wronged. He then offered his exposition of the law, which the trial judge resisted on the basis that "extraneous matter was being unnecessarily introduced". The remainder of his long address was blatant rhetoric.

Barry summed up to the jury that the conduct of Dr Lang had been reprehensible in making his appeal directly to the public, rather than by using available legal remedies, including the possibility of seeking a new trial. He "decanted on the subject matter of the libel", pointing out "several severe strictures" that had been applied to the character of the Chief Justice, especially those suggesting that a'Beckett had wilfully misdirected the jurors and that the latter had violated the oaths under which they had served. He made much of the contemptuous effect of the comparison drawn between the conduct of the Chief Justice and that of Judge Jeffreys, for which purposes he read to the jury "Macaulay's life-like picture of that monster".[68] The jury, in a few minutes, showed their complete disdain for the judicial advice they had been given and returned a verdict of acquittal which was received by applause in the court. The *Argus* observed the result with great satisfaction, reporting that:

> Dr Lang's defence . . . was really a masterpiece of art. In reading that speech . . . you are compelled to place the Chief Justice in the dock, and Dr Lang in the position of the prosecutor, and you are forced to the conclusion that the verdict of the jury is against the Chief Justice. It will be a long time . . . before the latter regains his influence over Melbourne juries.[69]

The *Melbourne Morning Herald*, however, spoke up for the Chief Justice, deploring the success with which Dr Lang had managed to "eject his venom against Sir William a'Beckett and the twelve jurymen who convicted the son". It maintained that "so much has been fabricated out of defeat and ignominy" and that Lang had brought the administration of justice into contempt "by the reckless vituperation in which he has thought proper to indulge". It failed to see how the "great cause of self-government" could be "promoted by the abuse of a Chief Justice".[70]

For his part, Lang was boundlessly jubilant. He wrote to his wife that, for him, it was a case of "*veni, vidi, vici*". He had, he said, in his two-hour speech, shown up a'Beckett "in pretty strong colours, as far as his principles of justice are concerned". Altogether, he thought the verdict "thoroughly damaging . . . for the unjust judge and [it] must be mortifying in the extreme to the whole gang". He exulted in his "great and signal triumph".[71]

In all of this, the power of the press, and the pulling of political strings, prevailed. It was a case of a demagogue, as Dr Lang was, laughing the law to scorn. The stark reality was that George Dunmore Lang and Drake, through misconduct and evident falsification of records in the absence of effective supervision, caused the Bank of New South Wales to write off a breathtaking loss of £11,000 concerning its Ballarat branch.[72] Yet Dr Lang had contrived to make his son appear as a martyr and the Chief Justice as a devil. It was the purest sophistry.

"Impeach the Solicitor-General If You Please"

The strain of the Eureka trials and of Lang's case took its toll upon the Chief Justice's composure and helped to augment his reputation for eccentricity and shortness of temper. Thus

Sir William showed the lack of sympathy, common to judges throughout all ages, for the non-appearance of counsel because of a clash of fixtures and, in March 1855, peremptorily rejected a solicitor's request for an adjournment because the instructed barristers were detained elsewhere. His Honour could not help that – "they ought to be in his court attending to their business".[73] It was in keeping with the Chief Justice's wish to press on with court business that he would, in another case, deplore "the amount of valuable time which the litigants ... were causing to be wasted". In another, he rejoined "Oh, nonsense!", to the suggestion of a solicitor, as a witness in a case about disputed costs, that settlement of litigation directly between parties was "behind the back of their attorneys". And, in yet another, he was displeased when counsel announced that, because the prosecution had occupied two days, the defence would require equal time:

> The Chief Justice: Good gracious! Counsel on each side seem in the *res gestae* to embrace all topics, conceivable and inconceivable, before and after the matter of the transaction. This is very unfair to the jury.[74]

In the criminal cases of Stevenson and Lowrie at the start of the 1855 sittings, Stevenson's counsel sought to have his client discharged because the prosecutor had failed to appear. The Chief Justice proposed deferring the matter to another day. Counsel begged for a reconsideration because "these are very critical times speaking commercially, and my client is being detained away from his business at much loss". The Chief Justice responded: "What have I to do with that? You can impeach the Solicitor-General if you please. Make your motion tomorrow".[75] To a request that the prisoner Lowrie be released because he had already been acquitted on the very same day on the charge of horse-stealing alleged against him, the following exchange was reported:

> *His Honor* (with surprise): Acquitted. When? Where? Who acquitted him?
> Mr Dawson said the jury had come into court and acquitted him five or ten minutes before.
> *His Honor*: Then I must have been talking to the Sheriff. If he is acquitted, of course let him go.[76]

The Chief Justice, in his own peculiar way, tried sometimes to bring a touch of relief to proceedings by resorting to humour that was sardonic and often at the expense of others. One afternoon, in

1855, Ireland of the Bar asked if a'Beckett would entertain further cases that day as the next in the list was a breach of promise action that would probably be protracted. The press reported:

> His Honor: Oh, let us get on; at any rate it will be more amusing than the other cases.
> Mr Michie: Unfortunately, the parties have kept all the amusement to themselves, for they have settled the matter out of court.[77]

The case nevertheless was called on, when it appeared that "the defendant had given accord and satisfaction, promising to marry the plaintiff today". The Chief Justice retorted: "Oh, by all means let it stand over; if they came into this court to litigate it, they will never get married at all".[78] In a similar vein, a'Beckett shared the notorious penchant for puns that had been displayed by Sir James Dowling when Chief Justice of New South Wales.[79] For instance, in *Bear* v. *Priestley*, in 1856, on the question whether trade usage could be proved by evidence in an action at law, Michie, from the Bar table observed, mischievously, that "Bear was strictly speaking not entitled to one farthing. Bear could not bring it to bear. (A suppressed groan was heard and several learned counsel shuddered)". The Chief Justice could not resist the rejoinder, "That is really quite un*bear*able". The ensuing decision of the Full Bench of the court seemed inspired with the same levity, being condensed into these words:

> Chief Justice: I think the parties have made their own contract, and that usage had nothing to do with it.
> Mr Justice Williams: I think the plaintiff is not entitled to sixpence.
> Mr Justice Barry: We do not decide that usage is in no case admissible, but simply not here.[80]

Incidentally, it was unremarkable that perfunctory judgments were delivered even in superior courts in those days.

The *Argus*, never missing an opportunity to take the Chief Justice to task, disapproved of his sense of humour and declared that "whether his propensity to joking is to be imputed to him as a fault or a foible, in connexion with the grave office which he [holds], we shall not tarry now to inquire".[81] The acidity of the Chief Justice's asides emerged at the trial of Seekamp, in the Eureka proceedings. After a clash between Crown Solicitor Gurner and Prendergast of the Bar, in which the latter claimed that the former had withheld information the defence had a right to receive, the following occurred:

> His Honor: You can't expect the suavity of a Brummel from Mr Gurner.
> The Solicitor-General [*sic*] (with feeling): Perhaps if Mr Brummell had been a Crown prosecutor he would not have succeeded in maintaining much suavity of manner.[82]

While the Chief Justice did not regard it as a laughing matter, one is struck by the stupidity of a party who failed to recognize a'Beckett's well known support for the temperance movement. In *Ward* v. *Evans*, the prosecutor, who had charged William Evans, "a respectable looking young man", with assault, made the following observations about the incident:

> *Witness*: I was not drunk. Am I drunk now?
> *His Honor*: No, but you are impudent.
> *Witness*: . . . The prisoner caught me by the throat. I was not so very drunk.
> *His Honor*: I never heard a man in a witness box admit he was drunk yet.[83]

Realizing the futility of proceeding, the Solicitor-General at once abandoned the case, and the jury returned an acquittal.

These, however, are matters of little import. They give no more than a glimpse of a'Beckett's demeanour at a time when he was pressed with highly controversial cases and a burden of many less spectacular hearings. To some of the latter it is convenient now to give brief attention. A number of them turned on the effects of the constitutional separation of Victoria from New South Wales. In *Hodgson* v. *Quiney*, in 1856, there was a question of title to land.[84] A Crown grant had been issued, before separation, to land in "Port Phillip", the grant being recorded in the registry of deeds at Sydney, then the only registry for the territory of which Port Phillip formed part. The question was whether a copy of the entry of registration, certified by the Colonial Secretary of New South Wales after separation, took effect in Victoria, having regard to Victorian legislation that called for certification by an appropriate officer of the Supreme Court of that Colony. The court, on analysing the enactments, imperial and colonial, reached the following conclusion:

> To say . . . that in the present case, the words "Chief Clerk of the Supreme Court of New South Wales", must be read as "Chief Clerk of the Supreme Court of Victoria", is only another way of saying that the Act shall be read in such a manner as to be perfectly inoperative;

> in other words, that that which the Imperial Parliament has declared shall continue to be in force, shall not be in force. It is, in fact, a misapplication of phraseology for the purpose of a misapplication of the law. Now, if we had to deal with an entirely new statutory code, incorporated from another country, we might find difficulties, as we do now occasionally in the application of that part of the English statute law declared to be in force up to the time of 9 Geo. IV.; but the continuance of the same laws in a country only distinguished thereafter by another name, and as an independent State, gives rise simply to a difference of nomenclature, and the cessation of any future legislative relations between it and the country to which it formerly belonged.[85]

In the earlier case of *Halfpenny* v. *Kinnelly*, the Chief Justice had similarly accepted a certification by the Chief Clerk of the Supreme Court in Sydney as to a pre-separation grant, but only as a secondary officer to the Prothonotary and Registrar of that court. The Chief Justice preferred a liberal construction of the governing Acts – "unless there is something distinctly to show that all deeds relating to land in the district of Port Phillip shall be enrolled here, and all other evidence of them shall be excluded, I do not think we should be justified in refusing evidence of any certified copy from Sydney".[86]

In *Strutt* v. *O'Hara*, in 1856, the plaintiff sought to enforce a judgment recovered against the defendant in New South Wales. In Victoria, the defendant pleaded that he had never been in the neighbouring Colony or held property there. After the court had taken time to consider, the Chief Justice delivered the joint decision that affirmed the separate standing of Victoria for the purposes of private international law. The court was satisfied that the defendant could not have been served with notice or process in New South Wales, and recovery against him therefore failed.[87]

There was sometimes uncertainty about powers vested in the Supreme Court of Victoria under the legislation founding it. In *Stephen* v. *Watson*, a'Beckett questioned the jurisdiction of the Full Court to entertain a demurrer to an information in libel. As he posed the question, "[The matter] originated in a Court which is in effect an Assize Court. How do you get it from the Assize Court here?". Counsel reasonably submitted that the Supreme Court *in banco* had all the functions of the Queen's Bench. The Chief Justice was not convinced that proper practice had been followed and agreed, only with reluctance, to hear the merits, reserving the right to repudiate any precedent if, on reflection, it appeared that the course adopted was prejudicial.[88]

In *In re Sherry*, in 1856, Sir William a'Beckett affirmed the Supreme Court's investment with the general parental jurisdiction of the Court of Chancery in England, but pointed out limits to its practical application. He observed that:

> The jurisdiction of the Court of Chancery over infants is one which is of a protective, and not of an inquisitorial or arbitrary character, and is exercised either to secure their persons from cruelty or ill-usage, or their property from waste or spoliation. In the present case there is no property to deal with; and the only question, therefore, is as to the custody of the persons of these two infants. The relations of Guardian and Ward, in the sense of those words as understood in a Court of Equity, do not exist in the case of these children, for the Court does not hesitate to say, that as regards them [the guardian] ought never to have been appointed guardian at all. There was neither suit nor property in respect of which such suit could be instituted.[89]

Another traditional power, which the court exercised zealously, concerned the admission and regulation of legal practitioners. In *Williamson* v. *Pretty*, for example, in 1856, there had been a trial of a solicitor, before the Chief Justice, on counts of negligence. The solicitor had acted for a former poundkeeper at Carisbrook, who was tried at Quarter Sessions and found guilty of embezzlement. Counsel had been retained, and he successfully moved that a case be stated, on doubtful points, for the decision of the Full Supreme Court. The trial judge was preoccupied with sittings in other towns and the stated case took five months to reach the Prothonotary's office. The solicitor had done nothing to seek expedition, and the barrister was absent from Melbourne. Meanwhile, the former poundkeeper, being unable to raise bail, languished in prison until seeking other legal advisers who had the case set down and argued, with the result that he was discharged. He sued his original solicitor for damages, the jury awarding him £300. The solicitor applied for a rule *nisi* for a new trial on the ground of a misdirection. On that application, before the Full Court, a formidable forensic team - Attorney-General Stawell, Whipham and Fellows - appeared in support of the rule. Stawell submitted that the solicitor had no standing to importune the judge at Quarter Sessions to expedite the stated case, and could have done nothing further to hasten a hearing. There was also an uncharitable attempt to pass any blame to counsel at the Quarter Sessions trial, which a'Beckett at once rejected – "the neglect complained of here was no part of the duty of counsel". The court discharged the rule, the Chief Justice stating that:

> The attorney knew that his client was lying in gaol, and that the only way to release him was to get the case tried. It is monstrous to say that knowing this, he can justify his neglect in writing to or communicating with the person who alone could expedite the matter, because there was a chance that he might get an unsatisfactory answer... In this case, an inquiry by the attorney of the judge would, in all reasonable probability, have set things right, and was a step which any man of ordinary prudence and ordinary skill would have taken.[90]

Mr Justice Barry unreservedly agreed.

Problems also arose from the application of new Rules of Court for the Colony, as in *Bakewell* v. *Francis*, where reliance was placed on English practice books for construction of the rules. In this instance, a declaration, framed under those rules, appeared to be at odds with the English authorities. The Chief Justice adhered to the colonial rules – "Great as is the authority of Stephen on Pleading", he said, "it is not conclusive, nor does it say that a pleading in the nature of a new assignment may not become necessary in a stage of the pleading other than replication".[91] Other difficulties arose when there were no governing rules, as in the case of funds required to be paid into court, which the Prothonotary habitually deposited to a special bank account attracting a small benefit in interest. The Chief Justice, in *Russell* v. *Burns*, in 1856, held that the interest was not to benefit the Prothonotary as a court officer (as fees of court earlier had been) but was accountable to the government as public revenue.[92]

There were related problems about the practice to be applied in the new court. In *Staughton* v. *Tulloch*, an action of trespass to goods, a'Beckett frankly admitted to having second thoughts about directions he had given on "a very novel replication" which attempted to show that colonial wool, seized in Victoria as distress for rent, was on its way for sale at a London wool market and was therefore privileged from colonial distress.[93] Sir William observed that "We must bear in mind the peculiar circumstances of the Colony. I remember, after the last trial, once I did doubt, in considering the pleadings as they then stood, whether I had not

Photographic portrait of Sir William a'Beckett

John Hubert Plunkett, Attorney-General of New South Wales

DR. LANG THROWS A BOOMERANG,
WHICH RECOILS UPON HIMSELF.

Cartoon of Dr J. D. Lang's attacks on a'Beckett (see Ch. 4)

erred in my direction to the jury, and required proof of too stringent a possession of the goods".[94] A demurrer to the novel replication was allowed. In the extended report of the decision published in the *Argus*, the Chief Justice further defined the limits apt to be placed on novelty in applying the law in Victoria:

> It has been the practice, and is certainly the desire, of this Court to act, whenever the peculiar circumstances of the colony are such as to involve parties in litigation, for the settlement of which no precedent can be effectually resorted to. But, though anxious to expound the law to the fullest extent that its spirit and principle will admit, we cannot go the length of altering it to obviate any particular case of hardship; nor, where a distinct issue has been raised at the point of contest between contending parties, can we distort the meaning of the language on the record for the purpose of giving effect to another that might possibly better meet the merits of the case.[95]

Perusal of the contemporary newspapers, and of the reports in the *Victoria Law Times*, reveals dozens of cases of importance heard before the Chief Justice and his colleagues of the Full Bench. Most of them turn on matters of law and practice now so stale as to make inappropriate any analysis of them in these pages. Nevertheless, one may admire a'Beckett's commitment to the heavy duties that then fell to the Chief Justice, and the skill with which he, as the principal writer of Full Court judgments, applied himself to the issues that the then law contrived to make excessively complicated. Rarely were there dissenting voices on the Full Bench. An unusual example of divergence was *Stewart* v. *Train*, in 1856, a case about the hiring of a ship. It was of such moment that it was heard before the whole Full Bench of four judges. The awkwardness of an even-numbered bench was demonstrated when the judges were precisely divided in opinion, and that of the Chief Justice prevailed.[96]

The commercial climate of Victoria, stimulated by the richness of gold recoveries, attracted litigation in which banks were frequent participants. In October 1855 the Full Court entertained a significant case *The Bank of Australasia* v. *O'Shanassy*.[97] The defendant, in due course, as Sir John O'Shanassy,[98] a powerful politician, made a move into banking in 1855. With others, he set out to found The Colonial Bank of Australasia which at once attracted the wrath of The Bank of Australasia, a chartered English bank since 1835, empowered to conduct business in "New Holland

and Van Diemen's Land". Its Melbourne branch had been opened in 1838.

The chartered bank sought injunctive relief in the Supreme Court. Argument of the matter occupied a whole day, there being a fierce contest. A very lengthy judgment, read by the Chief Justice and almost certainly of his authorship, was delivered one week later. The solution of the problem of a tendency to mislead would be left to a jury.[99] In practice, the litigation only promoted publicity for the new corporation which received much popular support and was affectionately known as "the Diggers' Bank". O'Shanassy was its chairman of directors until 1870.[100]

It was only to be expected that the golden age should bring with it abundant litigation over disputed mining claims. A notable instance was *Donaldson* v. *Cogden*, heard before the Chief Justice in 1856.[101] Cogden was a magistrate at Ballarat who had disposed of a dispute about encroachment on a mining claim. In the Supreme Court, the dissatisfied parties moved for a rule *nisi* for prohibition, restraining the magistrate from executing or enforcing his order. An order *nisi* was granted but, on its return, it was discharged, a'Beckett hoping that "future applications for prohibitions will be made upon more tenable grounds than those assigned in the present case".[102] Even an erroneous decision by the magistrate would not have attracted the remedy of prohibition. Either the magistrate had jurisdiction or he did not. In the latter event, there was nothing to prohibit. In the former, the circumstances showed that there was a decision lawfully arrived at on a matter the magistrate was competent to decide. In any event, a review of English authorities, which the Chief Justice then undertook, demonstrated that the magistrate's decision was not vitiated by error.[103]

Relatively few criminal cases called for attention by the Full Court at the period. An exceptional case, which went off on purely procedural and technical grounds, was *R.* v. *Melville*, the hearing of points reserved on a trial for murder of which the prisoner was found guilty.[104] The trial judge, Molesworth, J., reserved the principal question "whether I rightly received [specified] documents as evidence of the prisoner's being in lawful custody, from which he attempted to escape".[105] Melville had been convicted previously of other offences and sentenced to hard labour on the roads. He was conveyed to the prison hulk *President* and thence to the hulk *Success*. With others, he was being taken ashore from the *Success* under guard in a vessel under tow. He, and others, managed to take possession of the boat that was towing them and they overpowered and killed the boatman. Before the court, a copy of a warrant was put in evidence. It directed the prisoner's removal from one hulk to the other, but no documentary evidence established any authority for his lodgement in the *President* in the first place. The Chief Justice considered that to be a fatal defect and stopped the course of submissions from the Bar table. "This man", he said, "was sentenced to the roads. . . But there is no warrant or evidence to shew that he was lawfully detained on board the hulk *President*. It seems to me that there is a most important link wanting, and the conviction cannot be sustained".[106] The other judges concurred. Thus was the life of Melville, on whom the death sentence had been passed, unmeritoriously spared. The result, however, served to confirm a'Beckett's disposition to clemency.

Even the *Argus* was treated to constructive clemency when, in 1856, it published a letter by a steward at a horse race asserting that the owner and rider of a horse named Tomboy had deliberately pulled the horse up in a race it could, on prevailing form, easily have won. The owner and rider sued the writer of the letter for libel: the jury found for the defendant. There were incidental questions about a member of the jury entering upon the proceedings with his mind made up. But, on the libel point, the Full Bench hesitated when an application was made for a new trial. The Chief Justice gave it as his opinion that the letter was not of itself libellous:

> He could not say that a gentleman who takes a part in a public race as a public rider did not thereby subject himself to all the comments to which all public performers are liable. But it was not necessary to discuss that point, as he did not think the publication was libellous.[107]

A new trial was refused.

These cases do no more than sample the volume and quality of the work undertaken by a'Beckett in his closing years as Chief Justice. The sum of the cases confirm that the eminence as a lawyer he had enjoyed in practice at the Sydney Bar still continued. He was in his element as a judge of appeal and he presided over the Full Court with presence and authority. The elegance of his judgments, their powerful reasoning, and their careful regard to precedent, are features that may, even now, be admired. His judicial work at the appellate level was less well understood by journalists and commentators who mercilessly assailed his contribution as a trial judge, in which he was less assured, less committed, and more disposed to distraction and irritation. Hence his old enemy, the *Argus*, never managed to comprehend his true status as a judge and fell far short of the truth in claiming that "As a lawyer [he] was not distinguished as a 'full man'. But his learning, though neither copious nor precise in a remarkable degree, was generally equal to the demands made upon it".[108] Such a misguided assessment demonstrates that the writer lacked any qualification fittingly to characterize his subject.

"The Pettifoggers, the Tricksters and Hucksters"

Although his absence on sick leave spared him from having to wrestle with many of the immediate problems that followed from increased litigation, itself a product of new affluence created by the gold rushes, a'Beckett, as Chief Justice, was obliged to consider a number of abnormal demands being made upon the Supreme Court. Those demands, and his own physical limitations upon coping with them, played their part in stimulating his eventual decision to resign. Meanwhile there was growing frustration that legislation, passed in March 1856 to augment the bench to four, had not been put into effect by the government.[109] There was a clamour in the press that "all the business in equity is at a standstill". As was the case in New South Wales, though there in a more aggravated degree, the court's time was swamped by the demands of the criminal and common law sittings. Equity, with its yet unreformed procedure that encouraged delay measured by years, could not be accommodated. And that was at the very time when the community's rising fortunes created litigation properly to be determined on the Chancery side. Victoria's requirements were met by the elevation, as fourth judge, of Robert Molesworth,[110] in June 1856. Oddly enough, a'Beckett, whose experience would have fitted him well to adjudicate equity suits, took little part in that jurisdiction, unless on appeal, while he remained Chief Justice.

Cries for reform of the law and court procedure continued and weighed on a'Beckett's conscience.[111] While he seems to have had but scant regard for proposals to establish a Victorian Law Reform Association,[112] he was concerned to protect the public perception of the court. Many attacks upon it seemed to him to be unreasonable and uninformed, especially when made by groups as influential as the Chamber of Commerce.[113] In January 1855, for example, a committee of that Chamber publicized representations it had made, unsuccessfully, to the judges that the court's long summer vacation be discontinued to enable arrears of proceedings to be overtaken. The Chief Justice, with the concurrence of the other judges, dismissed the representations. Fluctuations in the volume of court business, he maintained, were beyond the control of anyone. The duties of the Victorian judges involved an amount of work "double that of any English judge" at a time when the labours of the bench were "becoming almost insuperably onerous". The summer vacation gave respite, not only to the judges, but to all practitioners and court administrators. Moreover, the hottest season of the year "in a climate peculiarly unfavourable to a continuity of mental exertion" lent persuasive support to the customary vacation.[114]

The *Argus*, editorially, attacked the memorandum. It was not necessary, it considered, that all the judges take a vacation at the same time. If there were not enough of them to transact court business throughout the whole year, then "the inference is that more judges are wanted, not that judicial business should stand still".[115] How could it be too hot for judges to sit in court, it mused, while it was not too hot for other business to be undertaken, commercial disputes to arise, and any class of persons to be wronged. Strange to tell, such compelling arguments managed to make no impression on the ordering of court calendars for well over 100 years.

Generally, the reforms thus far described had been directed to the law and its administration. In a'Beckett's latter months as Chief Justice there emerged much agitation within the legal profession itself of a long-continuing colonial dispute, whether the profession should be "fused" or remain divided, along English lines, into the categories of barrister and solicitor. In Victoria, "fusion" would eventually win the day, though its early practical effects were nugatory. It found no support from a'Beckett while he was on the bench.[116] Paradoxically, as counsel in New South Wales, a'Beckett had been briefed, leading Windeyer, for the applicant in *Ex parte Nichols* in 1839. It was an application for *mandamus* in which George Robert Nichols, the first native born Australian to be admitted as a solicitor, sought to compel a magistrate to hear him as advocate for a prisoner charged with having committed a criminal offence.[117] In an argument that called for the court not to follow the then recent English authority, *Collier* v. *Hicks*,[118] a'Beckett succeeded, and the right of solicitors to appear before magistrates' courts in New South Wales was won. The decision must have done violence to a'Beckett's private persuasions. Significantly, in 1841, he had been principal representative of the Sydney Bar claiming their right of exclusive practice at Quarter Sessions.[119]

By 1846, a Select Committee of the Legislative Council of New South Wales had to consider the consequences of an application by Edward Jones Brewster, an Irish barrister who had served for a time as Chairman of Quarter Sessions at Port Phillip until the appointment of a Resident Judge caused Brewster's holding of office to be suspended. Removing to Sydney, he could not secure a foothold at the Bar and sought to be disbarred and to have his name transferred to the roll of solicitors. The failure of his application, because he was neither a solicitor nor an articled clerk, has been canvassed in detail elsewhere.[120] Of present interest is the material placed before the Select Committee when Brewster, as himself a Member of the Legislative Council, tried to upset the Supreme Court's decision against him by sponsoring a private Act.

In representations to the Committee, a'Beckett wrote from Port Phillip, insisting that the legal profession was divided, not to uphold privileges of the Bar, but to protect public interests. There would be no savings in professional costs, he declared, if attorneys were allowed as advocates at the Bar, for they would equate their fees with those of barristers. Advantages of specialization, and of a better division of labour in preparing cases, would be lost. Above all, there was much to be feared from the increase of "police office attorneys". Most respectable solicitors would be too preoccupied with their rightful concerns to have time for advocacy. In any event they would not be the source of any problem:

> It is from the pettifoggers, the tricksters and hucksters, the flaw-hunters and sharp-shooters, the bloodsuckers of costs, the fruits of

> their own chicane or the errors of others, the pert and pragmatical charlatans – it is from these, the cunning, unprincipled, conceited, shallow, noisy portion of the profession, that the Court would suffer, and by whom the administration of justice would be degraded.[121]

That "admirable letter" was abundantly quoted in the editorial pages of the *Victoria Law Times* in which its editor, Dr Richard Sewell, adopted a'Beckett's views and embellished them with his own strictures on "fusion".[122]

Sir William a'Beckett's role in contributing to the founding of the Supreme Court Library was less notable than was that of Mr Justice Barry, but it was significant. The Chief Justice was on leave overseas when Barry made arrangements to allocate funds to establish a court library and, with a committee, to draw up rules for its use.[123] While in England, a'Beckett was given the task of obtaining, on "advantageous terms", the basis of a library collection. He augmented substantial funds at his disposal with loans from his own resources. At the same time he was co-opted, with his former literary associate Robert Lowe, to serve on a committee to make recommendations to the new University of Melbourne about the selection of its foundation Professors – recommendations that were adopted in 1854.[124]

One is not left with the impression that, as Chief Justice, a'Beckett was a powerful administrator, unless in the Full Court. Barry soon became the court's great driving force, especially as a'Beckett's long absence further diminished his contribution already handicapped by his indifferent health. On the Chief Justice's return, in 1855, court business had swollen enormously in volume and complexity, and he seemed sometimes distracted from and unequal to its demands. Other circumstances, attuned to the rapidly changing, and to him unfamiliar, character of Victoria, turned his mind increasingly to the prospects of resigning his commission.

5

"A Sort of Literary Mania"

"We Shall Not Have Another Milton"

This study would be incomplete without noticing the literary attainments of a'Beckett and his brothers Gilbert and Thomas. The most celebrated of them was Gilbert[1] who, while still at school – and after running away from school, joined in the enterprise of the other two to publish, as weekly papers, the *Censor* and the *Literary Beacon*. According to the *Dictionary of National Biography* those works "attracted much attention", though it must also be said that they attracted so little practical support that they soon perished. Thomas recalled that:

> William, Gilbert and myself were afflicted with a sort of literary mania . . . and brought out at our own expense a weekly publication called "The Censor". . . It brought us in no money, although for some time it paid its own expenses, but ultimately the sale fell off so much as to compel us to discontinue it as we had no capital in the shape of hard cash.[2]

Gilbert a'Beckett went on to greater literary things, teaming up with a school friend, Henry Mayhew, to produce other publications which, in time, led to Gilbert's being the first editor of *Figaro in London*, the precursor of *Punch*. Gilbert was an original member of the editorial staff of *Punch* – "shy, witty, ardent and clever, he was just the kind of supporting player that the stars of *Punch* needed"[3] – and he was one of the principal leader writers to the *Times* and the *Morning Herald*. He was a friend of most leading English literary figures of his day and, in the assessment of Thomas, should have been better recognized among them for his own creative writing:

> As a rule he confined himself to prose writing, but now and then wrote pieces of poetry which were really of a very high class character. His power of metrical composition was of the most wondrous kind. He seemed to be able to express his ideas in metre, as forcibly and as fluently as the ablest writers could express them in prose. It was, I think, only his keen sense of . . . ridicule, and his distaste for submitting to the eye of the public any verbal expression of exalted sentiment, that prevented him from taking a high position among the poets of his day.[4]

William, meanwhile, had been preoccupied with reading law, though he broke off from his studies to publish a book of verse, *The Siege of Dumbarton Castle*, in 1824, some of it written "during a month's illness". It confirms his standing as a writer in the sentimentally romantic style of the age, lacking spontaneity and having a laboured preoccupation with merely mechanical mastery over the forms of rhyming or blank verse. Undeterred, he published, in what has been described as "florid language", *A Volume of Poems* "by Sforza" in 1828. Before leaving for Australia, he contributed to *The Georgian Era* and compiled his three-volume *A Universal Biography*, works again much criticized for their jejune qualities, but which made up for a want of paid employment in court.[5]

He thus had a sufficient reputation, on his arrival in New South Wales, to be able to augment his income by taking briefly the editorship of Tegg's *Literary News*,[6] a Sydney weekly destined soon to go the way of the *Censor*. By 1839 he published *Three Lectures on Poetry* in response to "numerous inquiries", supposedly from those who had not been able to hear them delivered at the Sydney Mechanics' School of Arts in the previous year.[7] The *Australian* reported that the quality of the lectures blended together with other attributes "to augment our opinion of a gentleman who we confess has always occupied a prominent place in our esteem".[8] Yet, almost in the same breath, it criticized the lack of originality in a'Beckett's lecture on the poetry of Byron: "if the same observations had not, during the last twenty years, been bandied about from critic to critic, until they have become by-words in the literary world, he would be entitled to some credit for the terseness and elegance of his remarks".[9] The *Sydney Monitor* deplored the "many grammatical inaccuracies which pervade his work" and thought the "unfinished state" of the publication to show "bad taste". It believed that his efforts were wasted on a colonial community whose predominant concern was to make money, not "to cultivate the flowery bed of Literature".[10] The lectures, read today, do not appeal. They were superficial and platitudinous, summed up, for example, in the following *cliché* from his address on Milton: "it is doubtful whether we shall have another Shakespeare; it is almost certain we shall not have another Milton".[11] A modern critic has described the *Lectures* as "barely worth mention".[12]

Such was the want of evening entertainment in contemporary Sydney that a "very numerous and respectable audience" turned up at the School of Arts in August 1839 for a second round of a'Beckett's lectures on poetry.[13] He was said to have made "a vivid impression upon his hearers" and to have demonstrated his own "refined taste". Richard Jones,[14] merchant, Member of the Legislative Council, and harrier of lawyers, thereafter rose in his place in the Council to challenge the annual grant to the School of Arts as being a "useless expenditure". It was, he asserted, inappropriate that a publicly subsidized enterprise should be preferring lectures on poetry to "lectures on shipbuilding or upon general mechanical subjects". A vigorous exchange followed in which a'Beckett, in most un-Victorian language, denounced Jones as a "brainless bigot".[15]

In Melbourne, William a'Beckett emulated Gilbert's standing as a contributor of newspaper columns when he commenced an association with the *Melbourne Herald* as a writer under the pseudonym "Malwyn".[16] Perhaps the freedom of anonymity inspired him to greater poetic efforts than was usual for him, and some at least of his verse demonstrated the willingness of his Muse to adapt to the southern hemisphere. An instance is his "Leichardt's [*sic*] Return", the nature of which may be judged from this excerpt:

> Then hail him on his safe return, with one applauding voice,
> Who brings us news to sadden none, and all may make rejoice,
> Who comes to tell that, 'spite our fears, the grass does not yet wave,
> O'er any spot the desert holds that leads to "Leichardt's grave".[17]

It has been suggested that he contributed to, and perhaps helped to launch, *Melbourne Punch*, though caustic reflections on him in that journal would have invited a contrary view had not the suggestion itself been demonstrably untrue.[18]

William a'Beckett's interest was not confined to the great English poets, novelists and dramatists. One of his concerns was the alleviation of suffering among poor and downtrodden peoples, a theme he had pursued from the writing of "The Siege of Dumbarton Castle".[19] His abhorrence of slavery and his taste for good writing were alike stimulated when a friend lent him a copy of *Uncle Tom's Cabin*. In writing to return it, a'Beckett told more of himself than he ever did in any public lecture: "I have read [it] thro as it were, at a breath, for I could not stop, when I began it. I do not wonder at the sensation it has created – nothing can be more thrilling than its disclosures – or more powerful than its appeals on behalf of the wretched and oppressed race to whom it relates; but this is something more than a novel".[20]

Sir William also delivered occasional lectures on poetry in Melbourne. Probably the last of them was at the Mechanics' Institute in November 1856 when "the number of ladies present was less than might have been expected, owing no doubt to the attractions of the [Benevolent Asylum] Bazaar".[21] More usually his public utterances in Victoria were confined to temperance questions, on which he preached, as it were, to the converted.

"Beware of the Empoisoned Fruit"

In 1854 he published, in London, his *Out of Harness*, giving an account of some of his travels in Europe with his wife and sons during the sick leave he had solicited. It is an eccentric volume, of no special distinction as a work of prose, reading as if a catalogue of complaints and disappointments.[22] England offered him "six days' tears to one day's smiles"; the Rhine was "overrated"; accommodation on the Continent was hard to get and of poor quality; travelling connexions were missed; he hated rail travel; "not much" was to be seen in Basle; Milan cathedral was "cold, dark and vast" – the women of Milan were "*in*tolerably" ugly; the journey to Rome "offered nothing attractive in the scenery"; while Naples was beautiful, but "how very noisy and dirty are the streets. . .! How annoying the beggars! How nasty the habits of the people". The only redeeming feature of the tour seems to have been that expenses were, on average, contained to 15 shillings per head per day.

What emerges most clearly are the attention and devotion to him of his sons during the journey in physically carrying him about, for his paralysis made it almost impossible for him to walk. He wrote:

> I was carried on the back of one of my sons not only up the steps of the Colosseum, but up the steps of all other notable localities, both of Rome and elsewhere, where my curiosity would, but my legs would not, convey me. People stared, but not rudely, and if they did, what cared I? . . . I am afraid I did try a *little* the moral courage, as well as the physical strength of my sons in these decidedly practical illustrations of contempt for appearances.[23]

He went on, in 1855, to pursue his travel theme in papers contributed to the *Melbourne Monthly Magazine* – which, incidentally, ceased publication soon afterwards. In these he wrote of a second tour to the Continent in which he sought relief from paralysis by taking spa baths. He did not mind leaving London in the summer. He found the city much changed in the 18 years since he had last been there and, to have remained in London at that time would have placed him in an embarrassing position financially and socially:

> It requires both more wealth and leisure than were at my command to enter into all the enjoyments of what is called "the season". To go through the round of them, from beginning to end, one must be very idle and very rich. . . The fact is, when one has lived for many years in the colonies . . ., even one's native country become[s] to us almost strange and foreign.[24]

At Wildbad, in Germany, he took 14 baths, "with decided effect" according to his doctor, but with none at all according to Sir William himself.[25] The tour seems to have been no less depressing than the first had been, and there was little good to be said of anything. The weather was wet; the roads muddy; there was nothing intellectually stimulating; while Wildbad appalled him – "besides the one little dirty, contemptible street, the village consists of one miserable church" and three hotels. As for the bath house, he wrote, as if detached from the proceedings:

> Oh, what a dilapidated set of human beings were hobbling about from morning to night. . . It was painful to behold a collection of such infirmities; though I could not, sometimes, help smiling at the patient gullibility with which they went through the orthodox routine of valetudinarian discipline, prescribed by the medical *lex loci*.[26]

At the end of the tour he was overcome with "disgust and mortification" and "exhibited what people call temper", being disagreeable to family and strangers alike, and sulking during coach journeys, keeping to himself and refusing even to contemplate the views.[27]

Despite the strange and foreign character assumed by his homeland, he was destined, sooner than he could then have expected, to return there to live in retirement, in circumstances shortly to be noticed. As was discovered by many judges quitting colonial service when pensionable, England had little occupation and few charms to offer. The a'Becketts, on their ultimate return, similarly found that time weighed heavily, and that demotion from a leading colonial place to anonymity in Britain was correspondingly stultifying. Sir William threw himself into yet further writing, but his poetry of the retirement period was even more forced, ponderous and pedestrian than some of his earlier efforts had been.

In 1863 he published *The Earl's Choice and Other Poems*. The "Earl's Choice", he maintained, was "a tale in verse, rather than a poem" and it was the item that occupied much of his time immediately after retirement. He included with it some verses written in earlier years, adding, almost apologetically:

> During his residence in Australia, he was too much engaged in the pursuit of his profession to allow of frequent intercourse with the Muse; but although thus debarred the poet's vocation, the aspirations of one never forsook him, and resulted from time to time, in those utterances from which the present selection is made.[28]

He thought that some of the utterances might seem "too personal for the public eye" but, as to the book at large, he believed that "the friends who look for it will give it kindly greeting".[29] To be kind to "The Earl's Choice" must have called for strains even upon the strongest bonds of friendship. A modern critic has dismissed it as "sentimental, priggish and rather boring".[30] Such notice as it received from the contemporary press was no more flattering. The *Weekly Review and Messenger* of Melbourne found the work to combine sound moral tone with prolixity of manner, and, while detecting a "pleasant impression" stimulated by the writer's "fresh and generous feeling", nevertheless thought the writing "level and unadorned" and concluded that: "As no attempt has been made to invest the subject with the charm of fancy, it would surely have been better to treat of it in prose. The author writes at an unnecessary disadvantage who imposes upon himself the shackles of verse without relieving them by the graces of imagination".[31]

Among the items too personal for the public eye was a poem "Under the Cypress", a memorial to his first wife, and a segment *"In Memoriam Fratris"* written in remembrance of his late brother Gilbert.[32] There were the conventional reflections of English writers on the reversal of the seasons in the antipodes, as in his "Christmas in Australia". And there was some hackneyed patriotism in his "Advance Victoria" with its moral undertone disapproving of the undisciplined state of colonial politics:

> Advance Victoria! May'st thou be
>   As good and great as thou art free;
> Beware of the empoisoned fruit
>   That springs from Faction's deadly root.

Sir James Martin, sometime Premier and, later, Chief Justice of New South Wales, himself well experienced in the creation of literary journals and in journalism generally, said that he had had "frequent opportunities for recognizing and admiring the highly cultivated taste for literature, apart from law, which distinguished" a'Beckett.[33] Another contemporary, Edmund Finn, who used the *nom de plume* "Garryowen", depicted a'Beckett as a "charitable, tolerant and accomplished writer", but that view, as summarized in the *Australian Encyclopaedia*, is associated with the realistic conclusion that "his extant writings are of no great value".[34]

Two things, however, need to be said in justice to a'Beckett. One is that, in an age when people able to enjoy leisure looked much to parlour pastimes, the writing of "verse" was a popular diversion. The effusions of a'Beckett were no worse than were those of many a minor English poet of that time. The other is that, like his interest in the temperance movement, or his nurturing of fine blooms for display at a flower show,[35] a'Beckett saw literature as a vehicle to influence, for the better, public taste and opinion. One may not admire his compositions, but his intentions, at least, were well-meaning.

"Speedy Release From Office"

Even the most vivid imaginings of his literary mind could scarcely have prepared Sir William a'Beckett for the dramatic and sinister conclusion to his judicial career that, slowly and insidiously, would follow his return to the Colony. The administration of justice, with the weighty cases of public moment that suddenly occurred, was a sufficient load to carry in 1855. Yet, in the very same year, there was extra-mural trouble as well. In September, his eldest son, W.A.C., all but clandestinely married Emma Mills, daughter of the late John Mills, a brewer and ex-convict. Aged only 17, Emma was possessed alike of considerable beauty and a substantial inheritance. Sir William and Lady a'Beckett boycotted the wedding, which was loosely spoken of in some branches of the family as an elopement.[36] It was not just that the union was thought socially indecorous, the marriage of an a'Beckett son to the daughter of a brewer, possessed of a fortune derived from the sale of liquor, struck at the very root of the Chief Justice's temperance principles. While there was later a *rapprochement* between the parties,[37] the marriage probably played some part in directing Sir William's mind to thoughts of retirement and quitting the Colony.

Coinciding with so many burdens to be borne at the one time was a'Beckett's failing health. According to W.A.C. a'Beckett, "overtures" were made to his father that the time had come to stand aside in favour of Stawell. W.A.C., who retained a lasting distaste for Stawell and his methods, recorded in his family history that his father did agree to withdraw, "on the strength of a verbal assurance that he should not suffer in the computation of his salary, . . . but after Mr Stawell obtained what he wanted he forgot all about my father's pension, and never left any record of his promise to bind the incoming Ministry, which utterly ignored his claims".[38]

The matter was not, however, the fault of the "incoming Ministry". It had been disposed of at least a week before that change. Stawell had been Attorney-General in the first Ministry under Responsible Government, of which the Premier was William Clark Haines, sometime medical practitioner and pastoralist.[39] That conservative government was defeated in Parliament in March 1857 and briefly replaced by a much more radical regime headed by John O'Shanassy.[40] The replacement lasted little more than a month before being overturned by factional alliances that rallied again behind a new Haines Ministry.

Stawell was Attorney-General, under the first Haines administration, until 25 February 1857 when he succeeded to the Chief Justiceship. He had been fortunate and astute in his timing, and in asserting successfully the traditional English claim of an incumbent Attorney-General upon vacant judicial office. Had a'Beckett's resignation come a few weeks later, Stawell would have lost the Attorney-Generalship, and the appointment of Victoria's second Chief Justice would have been within the gift of O'Shanassy. Sensing the drift of events, Stawell was importunate in his dealings with a'Beckett. The proposal settled between them was that, on establishing eligibility to pensioned resignation on the ground of diminished health, a'Beckett would be entitled to a pension of two-thirds of his judicial salary, and that he would retire forthwith.

The Act constituting the Supreme Court made no provision for judges' pensions. Before Responsible Government, pensioned retirement from the bench was ordinarily permitted in the colonies after 15 years' service or after a shorter period where permanent disability had supervened. The *Constitution Act* for Victoria, 18 & 19 *Vict. c.* 55,[41] set aside a fund for contingencies, and a'Beckett made his claim for a pension under that fund, supported by medical evidence that, because of the effects upon his paralytic condition of "an exciting climate and mental exertion" his "speedy release from office and return to England" represented the "only chance of his life being prolonged".[42] He was otherwise ineligible for a pension, having served as a judge for under 12 years.

Such was the pressure then exerted upon him to leave office that the *Victoria Law Times* (which, incidentally, thought a'Beckett's resignation due "less [to] a personal shrinking from the burdens of office, than [to] a wise and affectionate deference to the wishes and persuasions of his relatives and intimate friends") believed that there might not be time enough for the profession corporately to farewell the Chief Justice while he still held his commission.[43] However, he was duly farewelled on 20 February 1857. By then it was clear that the Haines Ministry, in its dying days, was not committed to superannuating the Chief Justice at the rate he had expected. On 12 February there had been a meeting of the Executive Council, Stawell being absent, but Thomas Howard Fellows[44] – who would succeed him as Attorney-General – being present, when the new Governor, Sir Henry Barkly, was advised to make an Order in Council regulating judicial pensions on the condition of 15 years' continuous service, or of affliction with some permanent infirmity disabling continuance in office, the rate of pension to be "not exceeding one-half part of the salary appertaining to each such office".[45]

Sir William a'Beckett continued to press the government to adopt the two-thirds proportion agreed between him and Stawell[46] as a condition precedent to the retirement. But the latter had then relinquished political office and made no recorded attempt to secure a'Beckett's claims. In the result, a'Beckett was "allowed to retire" on the ground of declining health and was bundled out of office on a pension of £1500 representing only half of his former salary. In England, the Secretary of State regretted that a'Beckett's infirmity obliged him to relinquish "an appointment which he has held with so much advantage to the Colony".[47] That only went to confirm the shabbiness with which he had been treated at the end.

6

Returning Home

"I Ought No Longer to Remain in the Position"

On 20 February 1857, in the "Old Court", from which he had refused to budge,[1] Chief Justice a'Beckett took his place on the bench for the last time and was farewelled on behalf of the profession by Stawell. It must have been one of the most perfunctory addresses of its kind, lasting less than one minute. While the Attorney-General was reported to have spoken "with a voice unsteady, and sometimes nearly inaudible", the alleged emotion was not exposed by the tone of bare ceremony with which the brief remarks were uttered.[2] The Chief Justice, however, was pleased to think them "warm and fervent", and he must certainly have been impressed by the congregation in the court room, "nearly the whole of the Bar practising in Melbourne" being present. It was observed by the press that "the seats to the very back of the court [were] filled with gentlemen in Bar costume [and] all the other parts of the court [were] crowded by the general public".[3]

The Chief Justice, in reply, marvelled at the great changes that had occurred in the court during his presidency of it. He congratulated the Bar on its stature ("except in Westminster Hall, there is no part of Her Majesty's dominions in which a more numerous, intelligent and courteous Bar can be found than in Victoria"), and he mentioned some of the realities that had influenced his decision to resign.

> On my return [from England], I found the business much increased, and the labours imposed on me were greater than ever. The climate

> told on me; for, as you are aware, mental wear is much more telling in a climate like this than in a colder one. I felt, in justice to my learned brethren and to the Bar, that I ought no longer to remain in the position of Chief Justice.[4]

There followed tributes of a less artificial kind than those tendered by Stawell. It was, perhaps, of some consolation to a'Beckett that the *Argus*, while candidly conceding their past disagreements, thought the time opportune to tender grudging amends. It praised his contribution alike in public and private life. As a judge, so the *Argus* declared, his strengths had been in his rapid assessment of the nub of a case and his prompt exclusion of everything superfluous. But it could not refrain from some criticism:

> His patient attention to the arguments of counsel, and the ability which he possessed of thoroughly mastering the cases cited before him, however numerous or complicated they might be, would have been sufficient at all times to supply the lack of large original store, had it not been for a certain eccentricity of judgment, which sometimes led him to take an unexpected view of the law of a case, and which occasioned not a few of his decisions to be unsatisfactory to the legal profession.[5]

The *Melbourne Weekly Herald* thought him to have been a judge without bias. It appraised his "learning" as "various and well digested, rather than extensive and profound; but his perceptions were remarkably acute, . . . his judgment sound and discriminating, and his logical and critical faculties so admirably developed that he excelled most lawyers, in the accuracy with which he seized upon points in issue".[6] The *Victoria Law Times* concluded simply that "in losing [a'Beckett] as the head of our profession, we lose a good judge and a good man".[7]

There remained a contribution by the solicitors' branch of the profession. In March 1857 a deputation of Melbourne and Geelong attorneys waited on him at his home, when the President of the Law Society tendered an illuminated address signed by 60 "leading solicitors", and the Geelong representatives presented an unusual gold paper knife that remains in the family's possession. In responding, Sir William remarked that he looked forward to closer social acquaintance with the profession should it happen that Victoria would be his "final abode".[8]

Staying in Victoria must have had many attractions for him. His mansion "Clarendon House", in Clarendon Street, East

Melbourne, with its imported inclusions (installed by imported artificers), was not long completed and furnished in great style.[9] His sons were committed to Australian careers. An honoured retirement as a colonial celebrity would have had much to commend it in comparison with becoming yet another colonial nonentity in an English backwater. But his grant of pension had rested on the unequivocal medical opinion that, not merely his wellbeing, but his very survival, depended on his departing from Melbourne's "exciting climate" for the supposedly salubrious and life-preserving qualities of English air! He could not, he conceived, conscientiously remain in Australia. In that he was unfair to himself. The government had shown no solicitude whatever for him in the matter of his pension: there could have been no moral constraint obliging him to quit his established home and settled family. Yet he felt that he was bound to do so.

Those considerations may be augmented by speculation that he wished to remove from Australia to escape embarrassing consequences of his eldest son's quasi-scandalous marriage. Dr Niall has concluded of Sir William that:

> If he regretted the need to retire . . . he would have been consoled by the fact that it distanced him from the Supreme Court at a time when it was to be much occupied with his daughter-in-law's estate. Actions against her stepfather and others began within a few weeks of the wedding and continued, at intervals, for many years, with many fluctuations in the a'Beckett income as a consequence. Sir William saved himself any possible embarrassment by returning to England. . . He was disappointed that his son had given up his legal career for an idle life on the Mills inheritance.[10]

Balanced against that must be the consideration that Sir William and Lady a'Beckett would have found it hard to be cut off from all their children and grandchildren in Australia. And it is not persuasive that Sir William had suffered any embarrassment by his judicial part in Mills estate proceedings that had occurred before his son's marriage, or by having made an order for the issue of process in the matter in connexion with an administration suit not returnable before him for determination.[11] With the bench then at full strength, there could have been no occasion for him to be involved in any contentious adjudications concerning the estate.

"We are Tolerably Comfortable"

Sir William and Lady a'Beckett made the decision to ease themselves into English retirement, first by way of lengthy visits to the Continent. In 1861 they spent much time in France. Sir Roger and Lady Therry, lost for occupation in their retirement, remarked on seeing Sir William in Paris.[12] There, in the Avenue de l'Imperatrice, the a'Becketts had transformed an apartment with completely bare rooms into something "fresh . . . and very bright so we are tolerably comfortable", though Lady a'Beckett was fretful at having lost her wedding ring while bathing at Le Havre and feared, without it, that she would be "considered an unrespectable character" in France.[13] Sir William felt much restored by the climate of Paris and was preoccupied with sightseeing, evening carriage rides, and "the waterworks at Versailles". He recounted that:

> We find the living very good, and our apartments themselves also – and the lady of the house is very respectable and obliging – but there are hardly servants enough for the establishment and one knife and fork serves for all the dishes. . . The table is rather crowded – the guests chat together in the drawing room after collation and dinner – the terms are reasonable for me.[14]

By 1863 they had come to settle permanently in England. Sir William rented a house, first, at Surbiton and, later, "Abbotsville" in Church Road, Upper Norwood, Surrey.[15] It seems that he had under construction a home of his own in Norwood "in which he intended to end his days" but he did not live to see it completed.[16] Idle time was at first devoted to production of *The Earl's Choice*, in following public affairs, in the activities of the temperance movement, and in recreation by way of carriage outings. Following the removal to Norwood there was another diversion:

> Passionately fond of music, he was almost daily a visitor to the Crystal Palace, where at fixed times, there was a fine performance for an hour or two of instrumental music. . . He indeed passed in the Palace a very large portion of his life at Norwood, having obtained the privilege of the use of his invalid chair, which was only granted in very exceptional cases.[17]

Thus life ebbed away, agreeably enough at first, but Sir William was overtaken by "a long and severe illness" from the effects of which he died at his home on 27 June 1869.[18] He was buried in Norwood Cemetery, probably with little ceremony, for he considered funerals to be ostentatious and often insincere. He once wrote of his hatred of:

> The sight of the theatrical display,
> To see the sashed stipendiaries that wait
> The signal for their faces to look grave.[19]

There followed a modest acknowledgement of a life of great public usefulness – a few lines in the London *Times*[20] and brief notices by an Australian press that had little reason to praise, in death, a man it had so disparaged in life.

~~~~~~~~~~~~~~~

As with other early Australian Chief Justices (sometimes with justification, but usually not), history has been niggardly in its judgments upon the career of Sir William a'Beckett. His every weakness has been exaggerated, often in cruel caricature, while his every strength has been suppressed. The greatest misjudgment has turned upon his physical incapacity: as a cripple, so that view assumed, he must necessarily have been ill-tempered, erratic, and unequal to the duties of his office. The deplorable degradation of him by the *Argus*, when it called him "an utter wreck both in body and mind", has lived on as if invested with timeless authority. Yet when the contemporary records are studied in depth, a very different Chief Justice emerges, as these pages have attempted to show. Were a'Beckett reincarnated in his office in the twenty-first century he would be universally acclaimed and admired for his fortitude in attaining, and well discharging the duties of, the highest judicial appointment open in a profession that offers little court room encouragement to the handicapped.

It is all together too easy to attempt to pick holes in the way in which he comported himself in the Eureka Trials and in Lang's Case. They were exceptional proceedings in which any presiding judge would have been a target for criticism. On analysis, a'Beckett's part, even in those difficult public hearings, was not fairly open to many of the strictures contained in and built upon the rantings of the *Argus* and the *Age*. Likewise, his views on morality, temperance and the gold rush invite the conclusion that he was so fanatical about those matters, and so conservative in his
~~~~~~~~~~~~~~~

attitudes, as to have abdicated all judicial objectivity. But it is a facile conclusion: his behaviour in court, as reported in the very newspapers that sought to defame him, constantly demonstrated that he put his private opinions to one side when he was on the bench. The "charges" he delivered, at the opening of the Supreme Court at Melbourne and Geelong in 1852, were inappropriate, but they were isolated and not repeated. Otherwise, it corrupts the truth to suggest that his personal opinions on society invariably accompanied him to the judgment seat.

He was a staunch champion of developing in Victoria the best qualities of the English legal system, of which he regarded jury trial as paramount. To suggest that he dominated juries and manipulated their decisions is to contradict the weight of the surviving evidence. His own commitment to the jury system was confirmed in his address on the opening of his first Geelong circuit as Resident Judge in 1850, "If in Port Phillip or Victoria as we hope soon to hear our District called, the efficacy of trial by jury should become in any way impaired, the social fabric will lose its best, I had almost said its only, security".[21]

He persevered in his goal of setting high judicial standards despite the almost unchecked licence assumed by the press to attack him in circumstances where, with either decorum or propriety, he could not respond. The burdens of his office, in the conditions applying in early Victoria, would have tried even a judge in command of robust health. That a'Beckett managed to win the confidence and esteem of the Bar that had been alienated by Willis; to stimulate harmony among the members of the new Supreme Court Bench; to dispense justice without fear or favour while himself constantly maligned in public; often to maintain an appearance of good humour in the face of illness; and to take courage to perform his duties incisively and to the satisfaction of the great majority of litigants (when, for much of his career, he was entirely alone and without the benefit of consultation or discussion with fellow judges), speaks eloquently for his character, strength of purpose, dedication and resolution.

In writing of English Chief Justices since the days of Cromwell, Lord Campbell observed, "they have all been men of decent character, and most of them have adorned the seat of justice by their talents and acquirements as well as by their virtues".[22] Those are the standards against which Sir William a'Beckett's judicial worth should be appraised. While not without the foibles that are the lot of mankind, he was a good and decent individual, a lawyer of considerable ability, a conscientious citizen, and a faithful servant to his judicial oath. He brought certainty and continuity to the colonial legal system during unsettled times.

Although most of his professional life was spent in Australia, a'Beckett probably never thought of himself as Australian. As W.A.C. a'Beckett wrote of his father, "he was thoroughly English in his sentiments, likes and dislikes, and in love for the country of his birth".[23] Nevertheless, Sir William takes his place as an Australian pioneer – the founder of an abundant Australian family that maintains its association with the law and takes justifiable pride in its origins. His contribution, as a lawyer, in New South Wales and Victoria, deserves grateful remembrance.

Abbreviations

(Used in the following notes)
(Conventional abbreviations are given to Law Reports)

A.D.B.	*Australian Dictionary of Biography* (Melbourne from 1966).
A.L.J.	*Australian Law Journal.*
C.O.	Colonial Office, with particular reference to papers of that office in the Public Record Office, Kew, Richmond, U.K., citing class, piece and folio numbers.
D.N.B.	*Dictionary of National Biography* (Oxford 1917).
H.R.A.	*Historical Records of Australia* (Commonwealth Parliament, Library Committee, 1914-1923), citing series, volume and page.
La T.L.	La Trobe Library of the State Library of Victoria.
M.L.	Mitchell Library of the State Library of New South Wales.
M.M.H.	*Melbourne Morning Herald.*
R.J.	a'Beckett's Reserved and Equity Judgments.
S.M.H.	*Sydney Morning Herald.*
V.L.T.	*Victoria Law Times*, page references given in square brackets relate to numbers added at the foot of each page in the 1970 reprint.

Notes

Chapter 1

1. W.A.C. a'Beckett. "The History of the a'Beckett Family" (n.d.), from a copy held (1990) by Mrs W.A.K. a'Beckett of South Yarra, and quoted with her kind permission, 1.
2. I *D.N.B.* 31.
3. Quoted, Brenda Niall, *Martin Boyd – A Life* (Melbourne 1988), 17 and 218, n. 9. Martin Boyd, "A Brief Account of the Boyds of Kilmarnock . . . together with their Allegiances including a Full Pedigree of the a'Becketts of West Lavington" (La T.L. MS7764, Box 640/9), 33.
4. Niall, *ibid.;* (1993) 13 *A.D.B.* 235; Paul de Serville, *Pounds and Pedigrees: The Upper Class in Victoria 1850-80* (Oxford 1991), 195.
5. "a'Beckett", a genealogical summary in the possession (1990) of Mr E.C. a'Beckett, Barrister and Solicitor of Aldinga, S.A., and quoted with his kind permission. The various Williams were born, respectively, in 1519, 1540, 1572, 1610, 1647, 1668 and 1691.
6. P.C. Mowle, *A Genealogical History of Pioneer Families of Australia* (5th edn, L.M. Mowle (ed.), Adelaide 1978), 3.
7. Information in the possession (1991) of Mrs Pat Rose of Davidson, N.S.W., and quoted with her kind permission.
8. Sir Bernard Burke, *A Genealogical and Heraldic History of the Colonial Gentry,* Vol. I (London 1891), 145.
9. Niall, *op. cit.* n. 3, 218-219, n. 12.
10. A. Wood Renton (ed.), *Encyclopaedia of the Laws of England,* Vol. IX (London 1898), 41-42.
11. *D'Eyncourt* v. *Gregory* (1875) 1 Ch.D. 441.
12. Inscription by William a'Beckett in a copy of Giles Jacob, *A New Law Dictionary* (9th ed., London 1772), in the possession (1990) of Mr E.C. a'Beckett and since deposited with the Library of the Supreme Court of Victoria.
13. Niall, *loc. cit.* n. 9.
14. *D.N.B., loc. cit.* n. 2; Burke, *loc. cit.* n. 8; "a'Beckett", genealogical summary, cited n. 5; Arthur William a'Beckett, *The a'Becketts of "Punch"* (Westminster 1903), 16.
15. "The First Chief Justice of Victoria" (1953) 27 *A.L.J.* 209 at 211. Some of the instability was attributable to his suffering from epilepsy, T.T. a'Beckett, *op. cit.* n. 16, 7.
16. Thomas Turner a'Beckett (younger brother of Sir William), "My Family Memoirs" (typescript copy in the possession (1990) of Mr E.C. a'Beckett and quoted with his permission), 1; (1969) 3 *A.D.B.* 9.
17. Mowle, *op. et loc. cit.* n. 6; G.F. Russell Barker and A.H. Stenning, *The Record of Old Westminsters,* Vol. 1 (London 1928), 2; Alexander Sutherland (ed.), *Victoria and Its Metropolis,* (Vol. II) (Melbourne 1888), 457.
18. T.T. A'Beckett, *op. cit.* n. 16, 16-17; W.A.C. a'Beckett, *op. cit.* n. 1, 38-39.

19. A.W. a'Beckett, *op. cit.* n. 14, 15.
20. *Op. cit.* n. 1, 39.
21. A.W. a'Beckett, *op. et loc. cit.* n. 14.
22. T.T. a'Beckett, *op. cit. n.* 16, 5, 23.
23. *Ibid.*, 25.
24. *Id.*, 27.
25. Barker and Stenning, *op. et loc. cit.* n. 17.
26. *See* n. 12.
27. *Melbourne Monthly Magazine*, November 1855, 39. Four months of the journey were spent in Naples (Sir William a'Beckett, *Out of Harness* (London 1854), 83). The 1829-1830 adventure was made possible only through the patronage of a wealthy client of William's father – T.T. a'Beckett, *op. cit.* n. 16, 27 and 12.
28. (1969) 3 *A.D.B.* 10; Mowle, *op. et loc. cit.* n. 6.
29. T.T. a'Beckett, *op. cit.* n. 16, 27-28. The vessel was sometimes called the *City of Edinboro.*
30. *Australian*, 26 May 1837, 2.
31. *Id.*, 2 June 1837, 3. The occasion was colourful – "this being the first day of the second Term, the Judges arrayed in purple, took their seats in the Supreme Court". Purple was an unconventional colour for the robes of judges of superior colonial courts. Sir James Dowling, C.J., had introduced the practice in Sydney – *Australian*, 11 May 1832, 2.
32. *Report of the Proceedings Attending the Presentation of the Portrait of Sir James Martin, C.J.* (Sydney 1885), 11.
33. W.A.C. a'Beckett, *op. cit. n.* 1, 43.
34. a'Beckett to Lord Stanley, 27 February 1846, *H.R.A.* I/XXIV, 814 at 816.
35. *S.M.H.*, 31 May 1842, 4; 12 October 1844, 4; *Australian*, 2 May 1840, 3.
36. *Op. cit.* n. 15, at 227; (1966) 1 *A.D.B.* 216, 367, *Sydney Gazette*, 20 March 1838, 2 (and editorial).
37. The principal sources are referred to in J.M. Bennett, *In Witness Whereof* (Armidale 2001), Prelude, notes 47-59.
38. *Sydney Herald*, 16, 19, 20 November 1838, 2; *Sydney Gazette*, 20 November 1838, 2-3; *Sydney Monitor*, 19 November 1838, 2.
39. Gipps to Glenelg, 19 December 1838, *H.R.A.* I/XIX, 700 at 703.
40. (1967) 2 *A.D.B.* 264.
41. *Id.*, at 266; *Australian*, 27 October 1840, 3.
42. *Australian, ibid.*
43. (1967) 2 *A.D.B.* 609. The first Police Magistrate was to have been Francis Nicholas Rossi (*id.*, 399), former Superintendent of Police, but the office became vacant when he took leave because of illness.
44. *Sydney Herald*, 12 June 1841, 2. It is put, in (1967) 2 *A.D.B.* 609 at 610, that Wilson was "horsewhipped", but the *Herald* suggests direct physical assault in the dining room of the Australian Club.
45. *Sydney Herald, ibid.*
46. "The Diary of Judge Thomas Callaghan, B.A." (M.L. MSS 2112), 10 June 1841.
47. G.M. Dow, *Samuel Terry* (Sydney 1974), 225; *Australian*, 11 February 1841, 2.
48. *R.* v. *Taylor* and *Latham, Australian*, 9 February 1841, 2.
49. (1966) 1 *A.D.B.* 139.
50. *Australian*, 29 October 1841, 2.
51. *Ibid.*
52. a'Beckett to the Colonial Secretary, Melbourne, 23 October 1852, C.O. 309/13, f. 167 at f. 168.

53. T.T. a'Beckett, *op. cit.* n. 16, 29. *Cf.* Geoffrey Serle, *The Golden Age* (Melbourne 1963), 30 (note), which appears to be correct; and Sir Arthur Dean, *A Multitude of Counsellors* (Melbourne 1968), 29, which appears to be incorrect. Despite the affliction, a'Beckett remained an enthusiastic spectator at cricket matches - "Garryowen" (Edmund Finn), *The Chronicles of Early Melbourne* (Melbourne 1888), 739.
54. *Op. cit.* n. 46, 4 June 1841: the "fellow of the name of Steele" was the Revd Dr Thomas Steele. Emily a'Beckett was aged only 31 at her death - *Australian*, 3 June 1841, 3.
55. W.T. Cape to N.D. Stenhouse, 1859 (M.L. A100).
56. Fragment of a letter, a'Beckett to B.C. Rodd (M.L. A69), 12.
57. *Op. cit.* n. 46, 7 February 1841. Most of the barristers mentioned are the subject of entries in the *Australian Dictionary of Biography* - Plunkett (1967) 2 *A.D.B.* 337; Therry, *id.*, 512; Windeyer, *id.*, 615; Broadhurst (1969) 3 *A.D.B.* 234; Darvall (1972) 4 *A.D.B.* 23. Foster is mentioned briefly in (1966) 1 *A.D.B.* at 407 and in more detail in J.M. Bennett, *A History of Solicitors in New South Wales* (Sydney 1984), 50. Hustler and Purefoy were Irish barristers.
58. *Australian*, 25 March 1841, 2; Gipps to Lord John Russell, 20 March 1841, *H.R.A.* I/XXI, 290 at 291. Callaghan wrote in his diary (*op. cit.* n. 46, 25 March 1841) "I went to Court and saw Therry and a'Beckett sworn in: it was an amusing scene", but he did not disclose what made it so.
59. Dowling to a'Beckett, 31 October 1840, *H.R.A.* I/XXI, 299.
60. Stephen to a'Beckett, 11 November 1840, *ibid.*, 299-300.
61. J.M. Bennett, *Lives of the Australian Chief Justices - Sir James Dowling* (Sydney 2001), Ch. 8, text to n. 72.
62. Therry to Bourke, 21 October 1844, Bourke Papers (M.L. A1738), 735 at 736-737; and *cf.* Therry to Bourke, 27 February 1840, *ibid.*, 711 at 717-718. *See* also J.M. Bennett, Introduction to Sir Roger Therry, *Reminiscences of Thirty Years' Residence in New South Wales and Victoria* (2nd edn, London 1863; facsimile edn, Sydney 1974), [17] - [21].
63. *Australian*, 4 March 1841, 2.
64. Stanley to Gipps, 28 September 1841, *H.R.A.* I/XXI, 524; Lord John Russell to Gipps, 13 August 1841, *ibid.*, 468; Dowling to Gipps, 24 May 1841, *ibid.*, 379 at 380.
65. Stanley to Gipps, 23 March 1843, *H.R.A.* I/XXII, 592.
66. *Melbourne Monthly Magazine* (November 1855), 30; *S.M.H.*, 23 May 1844, 2; Ruth Knight, *Illiberal Liberal* (Melbourne 1966), 79; S.G. Foster, *Colonial Improver* (Melbourne 1978), 68-69.
67. *See* generally, A.C. Castles, *An Australian Legal History* (Sydney 1982), 228-237.
68. Section 4.
69. B.A. Keon-Cohen, "John Walpole Willis: First Resident Judge in Victoria" (1972) 8 *Melbourne University Law Review*, 703 at 711, 713.
70. *A History of the Port Phillip District* (Melbourne 1996), 182. Generally, as to Willis, *see* Bennett, *op. cit.* n. 61, Ch. 7. Willis, incidentally, thought little of a'Beckett as a practitioner at the Sydney Bar, dismissing him as a man "of very little, if any, practice at the English Bar", A.G.L. Shaw (ed.), *Gipps-La Trobe Correspondence 1839-1846* (Melbourne 1989), 127 notes.
71. Dowling to Gipps, 10 November 1842, W.M. Manning Papers (M.L. MSS 246/2), 81; (1974) 5 *A.D.B.* 207.
72. (1967) 2 *A.D.B.* 15 (Sir William Jeffcott) - of whom it has been said that the scruples became "of such magnitude that it brought him to the border of

insanity". John M. Molony, *An Architect of Freedom* (Canberra 1973), 60. On the other hand, Callaghan wrote (*op. cit.* n. 46), on 20 August 1845, that Jeffcott's head had been so turned by judicial advancement that "he began to cherish the wish of coming to Sydney to display himself and his law in the capital". On 13 July 1844, Gipps had written to La Trobe, Shaw (ed.), *op. cit.* n. 70, 270, that "you were right in apprehending that a proposal would be made to call Mr Jeffcott to Sydney – but I have resisted it".

73. Bennett, *op. cit.* n. 61, Ch. 6, text to n. 70.
74. Plunkett to Gipps, 23 October 1844, *H.R.A.* I/XXIV, 48 at 49; rejoining to a'Beckett to Gipps, 3 October 1844, *ibid.*, 12 at 13.
75. a'Beckett to Gipps, *ibid.; S.M.H.*, 16 July 1844, 2; Gipps to Stanley, 23 October 1844, *H.R.A.* I/XXIV, 42.
76. *Op. cit.* n. 74, 13, 14.
77. 7 October 1844, *H.R.A.* I/XXIV, 15-16.
78. Therry to Gipps, 5 October 1844, *H.R.A.* I/XXIV, 15.
79. Plunkett to Gipps, 23 October 1844, *H.R.A.* I/XXIV, 48, 49.
80. *Id.*, at 50.
81. Gipps to Stanley, 28 December 1844, *H.R.A.* I/XXIV, 151.
82. Gipps to Stanley, 23 October 1844, *H.R.A.* I/XXIV, 42 at 43.
83. Gipps to La Trobe, 14 October 1845, Shaw (ed.), *op. cit.* n. 70, 360.
84. Stephen to Gipps, 6 October 1845, Stephen's Letter Book No. 5 (M.L. A673), 202 at 204.
85. (1953) 27 *A.L.J.* 209 at 216 and (1992) 66 *A.L.J.* 872, respectively.
86. (1845) 1 Legge 253 at 264.
87. "Garryowen", *op. cit.* n. 53, 85.

Chapter 2

1. Gipps to La Trobe, 25 December 1845, Shaw (ed.), *op. cit.* Ch. 1, n. 70, 372.
2. Stanley to Gipps, 30 April 1845, *H.R.A.* I/XXIV, 327 at 328.
3. The prevarication was partly due to an obstacle raised by Stephen, in an effort to keep a'Beckett in Sydney, that the third judge must preside in equity. As so little time was then allocated to that jurisdiction, Stephen's ruse was transparent. Nevertheless, Gipps confided to La Trobe that, "if any effort be made to keep a'Beckett in Sydney for the sake of the Equity Jurisdiction I shall not interfere in it", 28 November 1845, Shaw (ed.), *op. cit.* n. 1, 369.
4. *Op. cit.* n. 2, at 329.
5. "Paradise Lost".
6. An opportunity also missed by Mr Justice Burton of Sydney – *see* above, Ch. 1, n. 73.
7. Gipps to Stanley, 5 March 1846, *H.R.A.* I/XXIV, 803 at 804; Sir Francis Forbes, Papers (M.L. A1381), 194.
8. "Garryowen" (Edmund Finn), *The Chronicles of Early Melbourne* (Melbourne 1888), 85.
9. Diary of Robert William Pohlman (La T.L. MS 10303), 7, 8 February 1846; *Port Phillip Herald*, 10 February 1846, 2.
10. Pohlman's Diary, *ibid.*, 11 February 1846; *Port Phillip Herald*, 13 February 1846, 1.
11. Pohlman's Diary, *ibid.*, 16 February 1846; "Garryowen", *loc. cit.* n. 8.
12. (Melbourne n.d.), 103. Similarly H.G. Turner, *A History of the Colony of Victoria*, Vol. 1 (Melbourne 1904), 262, wrongly suggests that a'Beckett's health had "demanded his removal to a cooler climate". Gipps confirmed

that a'Beckett was "extremely anxious to remain in Sydney", Gipps to Stanley, 5 March 1846, *H.R.A.* I/XXIV, 803 at 804, and 16 March 1846, *H.R.A.*, *ibid.*, 814.

13. Fragment of undated letter in "Autograph Letters of Notable Australians", M.L. A 69, 12.
14. a'Beckett to Stanley, 27 February 1846, *H.R.A.*, I/XXIV, 814 at 816.
15. *Readings in Melbourne* (London 1879), 3.
16. a'Beckett to Stanley, *op. cit.* n. 14, 816-818.
17. *Id.*, at 818. For the foreshadowed changes to the settlement - Geoffrey Serle, *The Golden Age* (Melbourne 1963), 5.
18. Gipps to Stanley, 16 March 1846 (Despatch 62 and "Separate" despatch), *H.R.A.*, I/XXIV, 814, 819.
19. Grey to FitzRoy, 18 October 1846, *H.R.A.* I/XXV, 222.
20. Therry to Deas Thomson, 22 May 1846, *H.R.A.*, I/XXV, 609.
21. *Loc. cit.* n. 15.
22. FitzRoy to Grey, 30 July 1847, *H.R.A.*, I/XXV, 693-694.
23. The Governor, however, had written, on 28 November 1845, to La Trobe, (Shaw (ed.) *op. cit.* n. 1, 369), "It must . . . be understood that I have no funds out of which I can pay travelling expenses".
24. a'Beckett to Deas Thomson, 7 May 1847, *H.R.A.*, I/XXV, 629 at 630.
25. *Ibid.*, 631. "Catalogue of the Principal Portion of His Honor Mr Justice a'Beckett's Elegant Household Furniture (who is about to proceed to Port Phillip)", T.S. Mort (M.L. 018.2/PA1).
26. FitzRoy to Grey, 24 June 1847, *H.R.A.*, I/XXV, 629; Grey to FitzRoy, 9 January 1848, *H.R.A.* I/XXVI, 165.
27. a'Beckett to Grey, 18 May 1849; FitzRoy to Grey, 27 May 1849; Colonial Office minute - C.O. 201/413, ff. 387, 382, 383.
28. *S.M.H.*, 10 November 1849, 3; P.C. Mowle, *A Genealogical History of Pioneer Families of Australia* (5th edn, L.M. Mowle (ed.), Adelaide 1978), 6; E.G. Coppel, "The First Chief Justice of Victoria" (1953) 27 *A.L.J.* 209 at 213; T.T. a'Beckett, *op. cit.*, Ch. 1, n. 16, 30.
29. H.F. Behan, *Mr Justice J.W. Willis* (Glen Iris 1979), 261; Sir Arthur Dean, *A Multitude of Counsellors* (Melbourne 1968), 12.
30. Therry, *Reminiscences of Thirty Years' Residence in New South Wales and Victoria* (2nd edn, London 1863), 353. For La Trobe's dislike of Croke - M.E. Deane, "Mr La Trobe's Perplexities: Choosing Legal Advisers" (1928) 13 *Victorian Historical Magazine*, 35 at 36; La Trobe to Croke, 10 July 1857, C.O. 309/1, ff. 292-295.
31. *Op. cit.* n. 9, 8 July 1847.
32. *Ibid.*, 17-19 March, 10 December 1847. Another such "fracas" was reported in the *Argus*, 24 November 1848, 2.
33. *Op. cit.* n. 8, 85-86.
34. *Albion*, 4 March 1848, 1. There was another clash, soon afterwards, on the subject of Croke's giving advice to the magistracy, a course of which a'Beckett disapproved - *Argus*, 17 March 1848, 2. As late as 1850, Croke boycotted one of the Resident Judge's dinners "in consequence of a dispute in court with the Judge". Pohlman, *op. cit.* n. 9, 22 June 1850.
35. Pohlman, *ibid.*, 24 January 1850.
36. *Albion*, 1 April 1848, 2.
37. Pohlman, *op. cit.* n. 9, 29 July 1848, September-October 1849.
38. *Argus*, 17 July 1849, 2.

39. For which she was sentenced to imprisonment for two years - *id.*, 18 July 1849, 2.
40. *Albion*, 4 March 1848, 1.
41. *R.* v. *Chessell*, *Argus*, 17 July 1849, 2.
42. 20 February 1857, 11.
43. Register of Remissions 1851-1852, inspected by the courtesy of the Librarian, Supreme Court of Victoria. It would doubtless have accorded with a'Beckett's private sense of compassion had he, in fact, caused to be delivered hot dinners to the inmates of Melbourne gaol "on Christmas day 1845" (Michael Cannon, *Old Melbourne Town* (Main Ridge 1991), 340). But he may be excused from such a public lapse in judicial detachment, on the ground that he was still in Sydney in December 1845.
44. 4 March 1848, 1. The *Albion*, however, met its match. Sidney Stephen of the Bar sued its publisher, Goode, for libel and won such heavy damages that the *Albion* was put out of business. The *Argus* claimed that to be an instance of a'Beckett's prejudice against the press - 21 March 1848, 2.
45. Quoted, *Argus*, Supplement, 22 October 1849.
46. *Ibid.* For instances of unrelated, but intricate, procedural points on which a'Beckett reserved his decision, note *Hambleton* v. *Smith* (1848) 3 R.J. 18-19; *Carrol* v. *Guillan* (1848) 3 R.J. 75; *Chessell* v. *McKenzie* (1848) 3 R.J. 96; *Jennings* v. *Corporation of Melbourne* (1849) 5 R.J. 2; *Ham* v. *Scales* (1850) 5 R.J. 45; *Mason* v. *Orr* (1850) 5 R.J. 81-82.
47. *V.L.T., No.* 33, 24 January 1857, 249a [498].
48. The clerk, Robert William Shadforth, edited the first five volumes - Alex C. Castles, *Annotated Bibliography of Printed Materials on Australian Law 1788-1900* (Sydney 1994), 4(18), 317.
49. The praise was unstinting because Stephen used the work in support of his own supplication for a knighthood, writing to Lord Stanley (6 February 1846, *H.R.A.*, I/XXIV, 757 at 758), "Your Lordship . . . will notice with surprise not merely the complication and difficulty, but the great importance of the questions litigated, and the enormous amount (in many instances) of the sums at stake".
50. A.C. Castles, *An Australian Legal History* (Sydney 1982), 247.
51. *Supplement to the Supreme Court Practice with Acts of Council and Notes of Cases* (Sydney 1851).
52. (1851) 6 R.J. 1.
53. At 5.
54. 3 R.J. 83.
55. (1976) 6 *A.D.B.* 150.
56. 3 R.J. at 89-90. In these proceedings a'Beckett had granted prerogative relief out of Term. The *Argus*, with whose editor the judge was in collision (below, text following n. 58) fired another shot, 24 October 1848, 2, declaring: "A better man and abler judge (Mr Justice Wills [*scil.* Willis]) tried his hand at the same "Star Chamber" practice and failed".
57. *Op. cit.* n. 30, 342-343.
58. (1967) 2 *A.D.B.* 50-51; Cannon, *op. cit.* n. 43, 332-333.
59. *Ibid.*, 252 at 253.
60. *Argus*, 15, 18 February 1848, 2.
61. 3 R.J. 31 at 34.
62. *Id.*, 43. The *Argus* confirmed its disposition to defame the judge by claiming that he had permitted "monstrous" injustice that "robbed the defendant of a fair trial and lowered the judicial office in public estimation", 17 March 1848, 2.

63. 3 R.J. 45, 46, 47.
64. 17 March 1848, 2.
65. 28 March 1848, 4; *cf.* "Vice versus Virtue" *id.*, 24 March 1848, 4.
66. *See* n. 44; *Albion*, 25 November 1848, 2.
67. 21 March 1848, 2.
68. 19 May 1848, 2.
69. An expression used by the *Patriot* of the *Herald*, 27 May 1848, 2. The *Argus* had attacked the *Herald* on 26 May 1848, 2.
70. *Patriot, ibid.* The *Patriot* pursued the matter on 5, 7 and 8 June 1848, 2.
71. *Op. cit. n.* 9, 23 May 1848.
72. *Argus*, 1 December 1848, 2; *cf.* "Garryowen", *op. cit.* n. 8, 288.
73. Pohlman, *op. cit.* n. 9, 24 November 1848.
74. *Ibid.*, 5 December 1848.
75. *See* also n. 63 for other objections to the rule.
76. *Argus*, 27 March 1849, 4.
77. *Id.*, 27 March 1849, 2; 6 April 1849, 2.
78. *Id.*, 6 April 1849, 2. As to Wilson, Serle, *op. cit.* n. 17, 18-19.
79. *Argus*, 10, 13 April 1849, 2.
80. *Op. cit.* n. 9, 14 April 1849; and *Argus*, 24 April 1849, 2.
81. 17 April 1849, 2.
82. *Argus*, 4 May 1849, 2.
83. *Id.*, 1 December 1848, 2; Alan Gross, *Charles Joseph La Trobe* (Melbourne 1956), 79-80.
84. *Op. cit.* n. 30, 343.
85. A detailed treatment of the portion of the case that commanded Jeffcott's attention is in B.A. Keon-Cohen, "William Jeffcott and Roger Therry: Two Judges in New South Wales 1829-1859" (LL.M. thesis, University of Melbourne 1974), from 151. *See* also, Coppel, *op. cit.* n. 28, 210.
86. *S.M.H.*, 25 November 1845, 2.
87. *Sub nom. Marchioness of Bute* v. *Mason* (1849) 7 Moo. P.C. 1 [13 E.R. 779]. Special leave was necessary as there was no automatic appeal from the Supreme Court to the Privy Council, an Order in Council permitting direct appeals not being made until November 1850 – J.M. Bennett, *A History of the Supreme Court of New South Wales* (Sydney 1974), 170.
88. 1 R.J. at 64.
89. *Id.*, at 65. For another instance of a'Beckett's preference to adopt a course better suited to colonial circumstances than were English provisions, *see* Castles, *op. cit.* n. 50, 454.
90. *Ibid.*
91. 1 R.J. at 69. Inconsistently, the same Sydney Bench issued a writ of *certiorari* on one occasion to the Resident Judge "thus establishing two propositions that the court for the district of Port Phillip is independent of that for New South Wales and at the same time its inferior" – Report of Crown Law Officers, 29 September 1851, quoted J.M. Bennett and Alex C. Castles, *A Source Book of Australian Legal History* (Sydney 1979), 134.
92. *Op. cit.* n. 28, at 210.
93. 1 R.J. at 71.
94. *Macdermott* v. *Develin* (1845) 1 Legge 243 at 244.
95. *Id.*, headnote.

Chapter 3

1. Edward Sweetman, *Constitutional Development of Victoria* (Melbourne n.d.), 25.
2. "An Act for the Better Government of Her Majesty's Australian Colonies" (13 & 14 *Vict. c.* 59); R.D. Lumb, *The Constitutions of the Australian States* (Brisbane, 2nd ed. 1965), 26.
3. John M. Ward, *Earl Grey and the Australian Colonies 1846-1857* (Melbourne 1958), Ch. III; Sweetman, *op. cit.* n. 1, 29-30.
4. H.G. Turner, *A History of the Colony of Victoria*, Vol. 1 (Melbourne 1904), 300; G.W. Rusden, *History of Australia*, Vol. II (London 1883), 484-485.
5. Paul de Serville, *Port Phillip Gentlemen* (Melbourne 1980), 31.
6. From at least 1840 - *Australian*, 25 April 1840, 2.
7. *S.M.H.*, 13 September 1844, 3.
8. *Argus*, 5 February 1855, 6.
9. "Garryowen" (Edmund Finn), *The Chronicles of Early Melbourne* (Melbourne 1888), 739.
10. *Argus*, 7 April 1852, 5.
11. *Id.*, 14 December 1854, 6.
12. *The Beacon*, "A History of the Melbourne Unitarian Church 1852-1952", 10.
13. *Argus*, 1 February 1855, 6.
14. "Unitarian beliefs ranging as they did from liberal Christianity to agnostic humanism were regarded at this time with horror by many members of the Anglican Church", Clifford Pannam, *Sir William's Muse* (Melbourne 1992), 52-53.
15. *Op. cit.* n. 18.
16. Report from Select Committee on Education (1852/53) *Votes & Proceedings (Legislative Council, Victoria)*, Vol. 2, 112-113; Geoffrey Serle, *The Golden Age* (Melbourne 1963), 348.
17. *Argus*, 27 January 1853, 5; *cf. id.*, 2 June 1852, 2.
18. *Does the Discovery of Gold in Victoria Viewed in Relation to its Moral and Social Effects, as Hitherto Developed, Deserve to be Considered a National Blessing, or a National Curse?* (Melbourne 1852). For a'Beckett's public "charge" to a jury, on the subject, *see* below, text following n. 41.
19. *Ibid.*
20. *Op. cit.* n. 16, 31.
21. C.M.H. Clark, *A History of Australia*, Vol. III (Melbourne 1973), 156, 189; Vol. IV (Melbourne 1978), 70.
22. Colonial Office minutes, and Pakington to La Trobe, 1 May 1852, C.O. 309/2, ff. 190, 191.
23. a'Beckett to the Colonial Secretary, 19 July 1851, *ibid.*, ff. 209, 211.
24. *Ibid.*, f. 212.
25. Pakington to La Trobe, 1 May 1852, *id.*, f. 193a; warrant for commission at C.O. 381/79, f. 72.
26. La Trobe to Grey, 22 October 1851, C.O. 309/2, f. 187 at f. 189a.
27. Report of Crown Law Officers, 29 September 1851, quoted J.M. Bennett and Alex C. Castles, *A Source Book of Australian Legal History* (Sydney 1979), 134 at 135.
28. *Ibid.*
29. *See* also, *Argus*, 22 January 1852, 2.
30. (1969) 3 *A.D.B.* 108.
31. (1976) 6 *A.D.B.* 403.

32. *Argus*, 3 February 1852, 3.
33. Dr E.G. Coppel, "The First Chief Justice of Victoria" (1953) 27 *A.L.J.* 209 at 211.
34. *Cf.* the *Supreme Court (Administration) Act* 1852, s. 3.
35. *Victorian Government Gazette*, 2 August 1852.
36. C.O. 381/79, f. 72.
37. William a'Beckett, *The Magistrates' Manual for the Colony of Victoria Containing Practical Directions to Justices of the Peace, in the performance of their duties, as required by Jervis's Acts, and the New South Wales Act of Council 14th Vic. No. 43* (Melbourne 1852); for a more extensive commentary, *see* Pannam, *op. cit.* n. 14, 63-65.
38. *Readings in Melbourne* (London 1879), 37, 38.
39. *Argus*, 31 January 1852, 2.
40. *Id.*, 3 February 1852, 3.
41. *Geelong Advertiser*, quoted in *Argus*, 24 February 1852, 2.
42. *Argus*, 11 February 1852, 2.
43. *Id.*, 22, 28 January 1852, 2.
44. *Id.*, 11 February 1852, 2.
45. *Id.*, 13 February 1852, 2. On the other hand, the *Melbourne Morning Herald*, which ordinarily sided with a'Beckett, considered the "charge" to be a valuable offering in "eloquent and forcible language" – 12 February 1852, 2.
46. *Argus*, 14 February 1852, 2.
47. *Ibid.*
48. *Id.*, 18 February 1852, 2, and "The Judge's Charge", letter to the *Argus*, 24 February 1852, 3.
49. *Id.*, 23 February 1852, 2.
50. 20 February 1852, 2.
51. Quoted, *Argus*, 24 February 1852, 2.
52. *Argus*, 16 June 1852, 5.
53. *Id.*, 4 May 1852, 2; *cf. id.*, 15 January 1855, 5, 9 March 1855, 5.
54. *Id.*, 1 July 1852, 5.
55. *Id.*, 11 February 1852, 2.
56. For example, *Patterson* v. *O'Brien* (1856) 1 *V.L.T.* 11 at 12 [22 at 23].
57. *Argus*, 11 November 1852, 5.
58. *Id.*, 13, 16 March 1852, 3.
59. *Id.*, 13 March 1852, 3.
60. *Id.*, 7 April 1852, 4. For a rule to reduce the damages from £100 to 40 shillings – *id.*, 5 June 1852, 2.
61. *Id.*, 16 August 1852, 5.
62. *R.* v. *Johnson*, *Argus*, 6 March 1852, 2.
63. *Argus*, 5 June 1852, 2.
64. *See*, for example, above Ch. 2, text to n. 42, 43.
65. J.M. Bennett, *Lives of the Australian Chief Justices – Sir James Dowling* (Sydney 2001), Ch. 4.
66. Certificate of Dr D. Thomas, 23 October 1852, C.O. 309/13, f. 166.
67. a'Beckett to the Colonial Secretary, 23 October 1852, *ibid.*, f. 167a.
68. *Ibid.*, ff. 168-168a.
69. *Argus*, 19 January 1853, 4.
70. *Id.*, 10 January 1853, 5; *cf. id.*, 24 February 1853, 4.
71. La Trobe to Pakington, 25 January 1853, C.O. 309/13, ff. 159-159a: at the Colonial Office Merivale considered it "a strong case", minute at f. 160a. *Cf.* La Trobe to the Duke of Newcastle, 20 May 1853, C.O. 309/15, f. 326, where

La Trobe stated that he had acted out of regard for "nothing but a due consideration of the Chief Justice's state of health, and the urgency of the case".

72. a'Beckett to the Colonial Secretary, 26 December 1852, *ibid.*, ff. 170a-171.
73. Michie, *op. cit.* n. 38, 37-38. F.P. Labilliere, *Early History of the Colony of Victoria*, Vol. 2 (London 1878), 342, described the matter differently: "on arriving in Melbourne, [Darvall] in vain went the round of hotels and boarding-houses, in search of a room for the night, and had at last to content himself with sleeping in an armchair in the Melbourne Club. He determined to decline the judgeship, and returned by the first steamer to Sydney". The *Argus*, 1 January 1853, 5, gave an even more colourful description, concluding that "Don Juan making his exit, carried off by the prince of flames, was nothing to Mr Darvall making his escape in the *Warata*". As to Darvall, (1972) 4 *A.D.B.* 23.
74. *Argus*, 4 February 1853, 5.
75. *Ibid.*
76. *Id.*, 10 January 1853, 5. The patent was dated 24 November 1852, Coppel, *op. cit.* n. 33, 211.
77. For example, Serle, *op. cit.* n. 16, 310.
78. 4 August 1852, C.O. 309/6, ff. 245a-246.
79. Minute paper, *ibid.*, f. 246a.
80. For Gilbert a'Beckett, *see* below, Ch. 5. Gilbert was reprimanded by the Colonial Office for making the application as his brother's "agent", the only agent recognized by that office being the Governor (M.L. A2358 - Victorian Despatches, 454). Nevertheless, his audacity was timely and well rewarded
81. 13 December 1852, Deas Thomson Papers (M.L. A1531), Vol. 3, 688 at 692-693.
82. Alan Gross, *Charles Joseph La Trobe* (Melbourne 1956). Similarly a'Beckett is not noticed in Council of the State Library of Victoria, *La Trobe and His Circle* (Melbourne 1989), and is noticed only in passing in Davis McCaughey and others, *Victoria's Colonial Governors* (Melbourne 1993), 28.
83. And told him so, La Trobe to Croke, 10 July 1857, C.O. 309/1, ff. 292-295; and M.E. Deane, *op. cit.* Ch. 2, n. 30.
84. Diary of Robert Pohlman (La T.L. MS 10303), 18 December 1847.
85. *Argus*, 9 December 1853, 5.
86. He did not depart from England until 6 December 1854, by the *Argo* – *Argus*, 7 December 1854, 4; *cf.* 26 August 1854, 3; a'Beckett to the Secretary of State (received 24 August 1854), C.O. 309/30, f. 10. There had been earlier difficulty with the Colonial Office which, at first, insisted that La Trobe had approved the Chief Justice's having 18 months' leave, whereas a'Beckett believed he had been granted two years' leave. The Colonial Office eventually relented, but pursued a'Beckett on the Continent, seeking his advice about jurisdictional questions concerning the Victorian Supreme Court - Newcastle to La Trobe, 21 July 1853, C.O. 309/13, f. 164; a'Beckett to Peel, 5 January 1854, C.O. 309/30, f. 2; a'Beckett to Merivale, 15 June 1854, *id.*, f. 8.
87. Sir William a'Beckett, *Out of Harness* (London 1854), 30-31.

Chapter 4

1. *Argus*, 22 January 1855, 2.
2. *Id.*, 8 February 1855, 6.
3. *Ibid.*, and 1 February 1855, 6.
4. No. 33, 24 January 1857 [483].

5. General commentaries are in Geoffrey Serle, *The Golden Age* (Melbourne 1963), 180-187; John M. Ward, *Earl Grey and the Australian Colonies 1846-1857* (Melbourne 1958), 286; C.H. Currey, *The Irish at Eureka* (Sydney 1954); H.G. Turner, *Our Own Little Rebellion* (Melbourne n.d.); Davis McCaughey and others, *Victoria's Colonial Governors* (Melbourne 1993), 53; and the item "The Case of Eureka" in the article "Martial Law" by C.H. Currey, *The Australian Encyclopaedia*, Vol. VI (Sydney n.d. - first Grolier Society edn), 3 at 5.
6. For the almost certain invalidity of the purported proclamation, *see The Australian Encyclopaedia, ibid.*
7. C.M.H. Clark, *A History of Australia*, Vol. IV (Melbourne 1978), 74.
8. *Argus*, 20 January 1855, 4.
9. *Ibid. Age*, 20 January 1855, 2 (Michie, for the defence, agreed, *id.*, at 3).
10. *Argus*, 20 January 1855, 4.
11. *Ibid.*
12. Currey, *op. cit.* (1954), n. 5, 38, suggests that, in Crown law matters, Lieutenant-Governor Hotham made the effective decisions (*cf. ibid.*, 45-46).
13. *Ibid.*, 78.
14. Sir Frederick Pollock and F.W. Maitland, *The History of English Law* (2nd edn, 1898 (S.F.C. Milsom (ed.)) Cambridge 1968), 503-504.
15. Generally, John Ritchie (introduction to) *A Charge of Mutiny* (Canberra 1988); H.V. Evatt, *Rum Rebellion* (Sydney 1938).
16. *Commentaries on the Laws of England*, Book the Fourth (Oxford 1769), 75.
17. A course much criticized by the press, *e.g.*, *Argus*, 22 February 1855, 4; *Age*, 24 February 1855, 4.
18. *Argus*, 17 January 1855, 5.
19. Serle, *op. cit.* n. 5, 174.
20. The Chief Justice specifically directed the jury, in response to their question, that the editor was responsible for an offending publication whether present or not (*Argus*, 24 January 1855, 5). A similar view was reached by the Full Supreme Court of New South Wales in a like case, *Levien* v. *Fox*, (1890) 11 N.S.W.L.R. (L.) 414.
21. Below, text to n. 54 and following.
22. 24 January 1855, 5.
23. *Our Own Little Rebellion* (Melbourne n.d.), 103-104. As to Aspinall, *see* n. 52 below.
24. *Argus*, 23 February 1855, 4; *S.M.H.*, 1 March 1855, 2. For the challenges allowed in treason trials - A. Wood Renton (ed.), *Encyclopaedia of the Laws of England*, Vol. XII (London 1898), 263.
25. *S.M.H.*, 1 March 1855, 4. The *Age*, 24 February 1855, 4, wrote, "Never in the whole course of our experience do we recollect such a one-sided charge as that delivered . . . by Sir W. a'Beckett"; L.A. Whitfeld, *Founders of the Law in Australia* (Sydney 1971), 128; Shirley Roberts, *Charles Hotham: a Biography* (Melbourne 1985), 164.
26. Lionel A. Gilbert and Elwyn S. Elphick (eds), *New England Readings* (Armidale 1977), 116-122.
27. *M.M.H.*, 24 February 1855, 5.
28. *Ibid.*
29. *Id.*, 27 February 1855, 4; *Argus*, 27 February 1855, 5.
30. *Age*, 27 February 1855, 4.
31. *M.M.H.*, 27 February 1855, 5.
32. 1 March 1855, 4.

33. 26 February 1855, 5.
34. *M.M.H.*, 24 February 1855, 5.
35. 23 February 1855, 4; 28 February 1855, 2.
36. 24 February 1855, 4.
37. 27 February 1855, 4.
38. Graham L. Fricke, Q.C., "The Eureka Trials" (1997) 71 *A.L.J.* 59 at 68.
39. *M.M.H.*, 24 February 1855, 5.
40. 24 February 1855, 4.
41. *M.M.H.*, 24 February 1855, 5. For constructive levying of war, *see Halsbury's Laws of England* (4th edn, Vol. 11, London 1976), para. 814, n. 2, which cites authorities, including some referred to by a'Beckett; and Sir William Holdsworth, *A History of English Law*, Vol. XIII (London 1952), 525.
42. 24 February 1855, 5.
43. *Ibid.*, and *M.M.H.*, *loc. cit.* n. 41.
44. *Op. cit.* n. 38, 65-66. There are other criticisms of a'Beckett by Professor Fricke that scarcely deserve a response. The fact that a'Beckett was a "conservative" figure (*id.*, at 62 and below text to n. 53) did not import automatic judicial bias: his "profound aversion to gold mining" (*ibid.*) was scrupulously put to one side at these trials (below text to n. 51): he was not "uncomfortably close to the Executive" (71 *A.L.J. ibid.*) and, after the proceedings in the Lang Case (below, text following n. 54) would have been very wary of dealings with it: the supplications he made for security of judicial tenure and for a knighthood (71 *A.L.J. ibid.*) were in accord with the common practice for all holders of colonial judicial office; and it was not a denial of procedural fairness that he addressed accused persons as "prisoner" (71 *A.L.J.* at 68), a traditional practice that continued in widespread use until the mid-twentieth century and was not seen at the time as being pejorative - note "Prisoners of the Crown", *Argus*, 7 December 1853, 3.
45. *A Multitude of Counsellors* (Melbourne 1968), 37-38.
46. *Argus*, 24 February 1855, 5.
47. Quoted, Dean, *op. cit.* n. 45, 38 (italics added). The quotation is from a report by G.H.F. Webb of some of the trials (commonly called the "State Trials").
48. Renton, *op. cit* n. 24, 263, citing 4 State Trials N.S. 414 and 7 State Trials N.S. 276.
49. *Halsbury's Laws of England*, Vol. 11, cited n. 41, para. 24, notes 1-2.
50. *Per* Lord Goddard, C.J., in *R.* v. *Steane* [1947] 1 All E.R. 813 at 817; adopted in Victoria, as applying to cases of treason, by Sholl, J., in *R.* v. *Smyth* [1963] V.R. 737 at 738.
51. *Op. cit.* n. 38, 59.
52. Butler Cole Aspinall, an English barrister by call in 1853, arrived in Victoria in the following year and was admitted to the colonial Bar. He was only 24 when he appeared as junior to Chapman in the trial of Joseph. Although a witty speaker, Aspinall played to the gallery shamelessly during the trial, making controversial observations, exceeding the normal bounds of advocacy, and reproved by a'Beckett as being "exhibitions of neither good taste nor good law". The same could be said of Aspinall's simultaneous prominence at public meetings, condemning the government and the treason trials - *Argus*, 13 March 1855, 5. A firebrand in politics, he later held brief terms as Attorney-General and Solicitor-General (1969) 3 *A.D.B.* 55; Kathleen Thomas and Geoffrey Serle, *A Biographical Register of the Victorian Parliament 1859-1900* (Canberra 1972), 6.

53. W.A.C. a'Beckett, "The History of the a'Beckett Family" (n.d.), cited Ch. 1, n. 1, 47.
54. (1967) 2 *A.D.B.* 76 at 80.
55. Serle, *op. cit.* n. 5, 178-179; *cf Argus*, 12 January 1855, 5; 17 January 1855, 5.
56. R.F. Holder, *Bank of New South Wales – A History*, Vol. 1 (Sydney 1970), 233-236, an excellent account of the defalcations, impaired by the author's willingness to subscribe to press assertions that "the conduct of the trial gives little impression of impartiality in the judge" (at 234).
57. *Ibid.*, at 234.
58. *Argus*, 12 January 1855, 5.
59. *Ibid.* Editorials supporting Lang, had appeared a few days previously in the Sydney press – Holder, *op. cit.* n. 56, 235-236; also the Sydney correspondent to the *Argus*, 4 January 1855, 4.
60. *Argus, ibid.*
61. In the then turbulent state of Ballarat, finding a detached jury would have been impossible. The Bank of New South Wales requested that the trial be remitted to Geelong or Melbourne, Holder, *op. cit.* n. 56, 234.
62. "G.D. Lang and F.L. Drake, Copies of any Petitions, etc." (1856/57) *Votes & Proceedings (Legislative Assembly, Victoria)*, Vol. 2 (C-No. 5), 15-16.
63. *Id.*, 18.
64. (Sydney 1855).
65. *Ibid.*, 48, 53; (1967) 2 *A.D.B.* at 81.
66. Serle, *op. cit.* n. 5, 179 (note); S.H.Z. Woinarski, "The History of Legal Institutions in Victoria" (LL.D. thesis, University of Melbourne 1942), 368.
67. *Argus*, 21 February 1855, 5.
68. *Ibid.*
69. *Ibid.*, and 10 March 1855, 5; *S.M.H.*, 1 March 1855, 4.
70. *M.M.H.*, 22 February 1855, 4; *Melbourne Weekly Herald*, 4 April 1855, 7 (pointing out that, had Drake alone been involved, the matter would have been treated as any other case of embezzlement).
71. 21 February 1855, quoted A. Gilchrist (ed.), *John Dunmore Lang* (Melbourne 1951), 584.
72. Holder, *op. cit.* n. 56, 235.
73. *Argus*, 9 March 1855, 5.
74. *Id.*, 2 April 1855, 6 (*Strange* v. *Walters*); *Regan* v. *O'Farrell*, *Argus*, 6 September 1855, 5; *Rawson* v. *McKay*, *id.*, 11 August 1855, 5. In the last case, incidentally, Ireland of the Bar cross-examined a witness, Horne, a solicitor, with the result that "the learned counsel commenced in his usual style of browbeating, but found he had caught a Tartar". Horne, having the last word, declared: "I have answered some of your questions a dozen times, and will answer no more. You cannot get the better of me by your cross-examination".
75. *Id.*, 23 January 1855, 5.
76. *Ibid.*
77. *Hackman* v. *Gessner*, *id.*, 9 March 1855, 5.
78. *Ibid.*
79. Referred to in Sir Roger Therry, *Reminiscences of Thirty Years' Residence in New South Wales and Victoria* (2nd edn, London 1863), 340; and *see* below, Ch. 5, n. 18.
80. *Argus*, 7 July 1856, 6.
81. *Id.*, 13 February 1857, 4.

82. *Id.*, 24 January 1855, 5; *cf.* his reflections on H.S. Chapman in *Amsinck* v. *Storey, id.*, 12 March 1855, 5.
83. *Id.*, 18 January 1855, 5.
84. *V.L.T.* [167].
85. At [169].
86. *V.L.T.* [104] at [106].
87. *V.L.T.* [345] at [347], [348]; reported as *Struth* v. *O'Hara, Argus*, 9 October 1856, 6.
88. *V.L.T.* [447]. As to practice under new legislation - *Bank of Australasia* v. *Hodgkinson* (1856) *V.L.T.* [59] at [60].
89. *V.L.T.* [137] at [140].
90. *V.L.T.* [42] at [44]. Note also, *Re Albert Read, Gentleman, One, &c., Argus*, 1 July 1856, 5, and *Regan* v. *O'Farrell, id.*, 6 September 1855, 5.
91. *V.L.T.* [70] at [71].
92. *V.L.T.* [479] at [480].
93. *V.L.T.* [281].
94. *Id.*, at [282].
95. 15 June 1855, 5.
96. *V.L.T.* [337].
97. *V.L.T.* [454].
98. (1974) 5 *A.D.B.* 378.
99. *V.L.T.* at [462].
100. *Op. cit.* n. 98 at 379. For the bank's future, *see* Michael Cannon, *Land Boom and Bust* (Melbourne 1972), 190-193.
101. *V.L.T.* [98]. The Chief Justice discouraged such proceedings in the Supreme Court and relied on recent legislation to insist that "all disputes relative to mining for gold amongst miners should be settled by the Local Courts", *Argus*, 20 June 1856, 5.
102. *V.L.T.* [102].
103. *Id.*, [100-101].
104. *V.L.T.* [417].
105. *Id.*, at [419].
106. *Id.*, at [422].
107. *Orr* v. *M'Crae* (1856) *V.L.T.* [279] at [280].
108. 13 February 1857, 11.
109. *V.L.T.*, No. 13, 2 August 1856, 97 [193].
110. (1974) 5 *A.D.B.* 264.
111. For example, *V.L.T.*, No. 16, 23 August 1856, 121 [241]: "In the numerous addresses now before the public from the various candidates for Legislative honours, every candidate tells us (as a matter of course) that he is an advocate for Reform in the Administration of the Law".
112. A correspondent, *V.L.T.*, No. 15, 16 August 1856, 114 [227], commented on a proposal to form a "Law Reform Society".
113. *Weekly Argus*, 13 February 1857, 5; reprinted from *Argus*, 9 February 1857.
114. *Argus*, 19 January 1855, 4.
115. 20 January 1855, 4.
116. J.R.S. Forbes, *The Divided Legal Profession in Australia* (Sydney 1979), *passim.*
117. (1839) 1 Legge 123. J.M. Bennett, *A History of Solicitors in New South Wales* (Sydney 1984), 64-65.
118. (1831) 2 B. & Ad. 663 [109 E.R. 1290].
119. *Australian*, 12 January 1841, 2.
120. Bennett, *op. cit.* n. 117, 59-61; Forbes, *op. cit.* n. 116, 47-54.

121. (1847) 2 *Votes & Proceedings (Legislative Council, New South Wales)*, 424.
122. For example, No. 2, 17 May 1856, 10a [20] and *Williamson* v. *Pretty* [42] at [44].
123. Anon., *A Short Account of the Supreme Court of Victoria and of the Law Courts and Supreme Court Library* (Melbourne 1969), 10-11.
124. *Ibid.*, 11; *Collins* v. *Supreme Court Library Committee* [1953] V.L.R. 161 at 163; G. Blainey, *A Centenary History of the University of Melbourne* (Melbourne 1957), 10.

Chapter 5

1. I *D.N.B.* 31; A.W. a'Beckett, *The a'Becketts of "Punch"* (Westminster 1903).
2. Thomas Turner a'Beckett, "My Family Memoirs" (cited Ch. 1, n. 16), 26.
3. R.G.G. Price, *A History of Punch* (London 1957), 38, 39; A.W. a'Beckett, *op. cit.* n. 1, 15, 17-18.
4. Thomas Turner a'Beckett, *op. cit.* n. 2.
5. E. Morris Miller, *Australian Literature* (F.T. Macartney (ed.) Sydney 1956), 28; and, generally, Clifford Pannam, *Sir William's Muse* (Melbourne 1992), 29, 32, 38-39.
6. *Melbourne Monthly Magazine* (November 1855), 29-30.
7. *Australian*, 1 January 1839, 1.
8. 17 September 1839, 2.
9. 14 September 1839, 2.
10. 13 March 1839, 2.
11. *Australian*, Supplement, 7 August 1838, 2.
12. H.M. Green, *A History of Australian Literature*, Vol. 1 (1st edn Sydney 1961), 119.
13. *Australian*, 20 August 1839, 3.
14. (1967) 2 *A.D.B.* 24.
15. *Sydney Herald*, 20 September 1839, 2.
16. The *Argus* gratified its dislike of a'Beckett by revealing his identity, (1969) 3 *A.D.B.* 10 at 11.
17. Quoted, "Garryowen" (Edmund Finn), *The Chronicles of Early Melbourne* (Melbourne 1888), 667.
18. *Age*, 16 February 1952, Literary Supplement; G.F. Russell Barker and A.H. Stenning, *The Record of Old Westminsters*, Vol. 1 (London 1928), 2; A.W. a'Beckett, *op. cit.* n. 1, 22. However, Geoffrey Serle, *The Golden Age* (Melbourne 1963), 357, identifies Edgar Ray as the founder and controller of the journal. For early instances of satire at a'Beckett's expense, *see Melbourne Punch*, 2 August 1855, 45 ("Sir Wm a'Beckett is quite incapable of ... partiality, but I esteem him as the brother of the greatest English historian – who is also the editor of the best edition of Blackstone in the language" [a reference to Gilbert a'Beckett's, *The Comic Blackstone*]), and 7 February 1856, 8, when *Punch* addressed the Chief Justice as "My dear Willy" and attacked his propensity for puns. And *see* Pannam, *op. cit.* n. 5, 51 (n.4).
19. Pannam, *ibid.*, at 29.
20. Letter to Alex Wilson, *c.* 1852, M.L. Doc. 1623.
21. *Melbourne Weekly Herald*, 21 November 1856, 2; *Argus*, 15 November 1856, 4.
22. For a detailed assessment, *see* Pannam, *op. cit.* n. 5, 7-21. That the editor of the *Victoria Law Times* should have thought a'Beckett's "style in these is so fresh, and his spirit so cheerful" does not suggest a comprehensive reading of the works – *V.L.T.* No. 33, 24 January 1857, 242 [483].
23. *Out of Harness* (London 1854), 66.

24. (August 1855), 227.
25. *Id.*, 292.
26. *Id.*, 292-293.
27. *Id.*, 349.
28. Preface, ix.
29. *Id.*, x.
30. E.G. Coppel, Q.C., "The First Chief Justice of Victoria" (1953) 27 *A.L.J.* at 222.
31. 30 May 1863, 4.
32. Gilbert's son found the piece to have "the condescending tone of the elder brother to the younger, . . . but it is neither displeasing nor inaccurate" – A.W. a'Beckett, *op. cit.* n. 1, 17.
33. *Report of the Proceedings Attending the Presentation of the Portrait of Sir James Martin, C.J.* (Sydney 1885), 11.
34. Vol. I (Sydney n.d. – first Grolier Society edn), 2.
35. *Argus*, 24 December 1852, 8.
36. Brenda Niall, *Martin Boyd – A Life* (Melbourne 1988), 19-20.
37. "Uncle William wisely accepted the situation with good grace", Elizabeth Chomley – Memoirs, M.L. MSS 4647 (4)(6), 25.
38. W.A.C. a'Beckett, "The History of the a'Beckett Family", cited in Ch. 1, n. 1, 47-48.
39. (1972) 4 *A.D.B.* 315.
40. (1974) 5 *A.D.B.* 378.
41. The corresponding enactment for New South Wales, 18 & 19 *Vict. c.* 54, provided, by s. 51, for seven-tenths of salary to be paid to judges retiring because of disability.
42. Barkly to Labouchere, 28 February 1857, M.L. A2345 (Victorian Despatches), 3941.
43. No. 33, 24 January 1857, 243 [483].
44. (1972) 4 *A.D.B.* 160.
45. As published in *V.L.T.*, No. 33, 24 January 1857, 249 [497].
46. Above, text following n. 39: and M.L. A2345 (Victorian Despatches), at 3942.
47. Labouchere to Barkly, 14 November 1857, M.L. A2362 (Victorian Despatches), 2424.

Chapter 6

1. The "old court" is described, and illustrated, in Michael Cannon, *Old Melbourne Town* (Main Ridge 1991), 150-151. By the time of a'Beckett's return from England in 1855, the court had been "entirely refitted" – *Argus*, 13 February 1855, 6. His preference to sit there was probably governed by relative ease of access, given his state of partial paralysis.
2. *V.L.T.* No. 33, 24 January 1857, 249a [498].
3. *Age*, 21 February 1857, 5.
4. *Loc. cit.* n. 2.
5. 13 February 1857, 4.
6. 20 February 1857, 11, "Political Retrospect"; *ibid.*, "Summary for Europe".
7. *Op. cit.* n. 2, 242 [483].
8. *Melbourne Weekly Herald*, 20 March 1857, 3.
9. Thomas Turner a'Beckett, "My Family Memoirs", cited in Ch. 1, n. 16, at 29. According to Dr E.G. Coppel, Q.C., (1953) 27 *A.L.J.* 209 at 214, "this house, which is a substantial two-storey building with arched colonnades in the Italian style, is still standing".

10. *Martin Boyd – A Life* (Melbourne 1986), 26 and Ch. 2, n. 50.
11. N. Long, "John Mills, Emma and the a'Becketts", *Overland* (No. 114), May 1989, 15-17.
12. Therry to Macarthur, n.d., Macarthur Papers, Vol. 34 (M.L. A2930), 83.
13. Copy of fragment of a letter by Sir William to his brother Arthur, 3 August 1861, in the possession of Mrs N. Allworth of Wellington, N.S.W., and quoted with her kind permission.
14. *Ibid.*
15. *Times* (London), 1 July 1869, 10; P.C. Mowle, *A Genealogical History of Pioneer Families of Australia* (5th edn, L.M. Mowle (ed.), Adelaide 1978), 6.
16. T.T. a'Beckett, *op. cit.* n. 9, 30.
17. *Ibid.*
18. *Times, loc. cit. n.* 15.
19. Quoted, Clifford Pannam, *Sir William's Muse* (Melbourne 1992), 49.
20. *Loc. cit.* n. 15.
21. Quoted in *Geelong Naturalist*, Vol. 1 (Second Series), No. 25 (1904), 5 at 8. For the inclination of Melbourne juries to make up their own minds – *R.* v. *Leigh, Argus*, 23 October 1856, 6.
22. *Lives of the Chief Justices of England*, Vol. II (London 1849), 95.
23. "The History of the a'Beckett Family", cited in Ch. 1, n. 1, 48.

Index